GRAB YOUR SLICE

of

FINANCIAL INDEPENDENCE

MONICA SCUDIERI

ISBN: 979-8-9863455-1-2 (Paperback)
        979-8-9863455-2-9 (Hardcover)
        979-8-9863455-0-5 (eBook)
        979-8-9863455-3-6 (Audio Book)

Library of Congress Control Number: 2022910102

All content reflects our opinion at a given time and can change as time progresses. All information should be taken as an opinion and should not be misconstrued for professional or legal advice. The contents of this book are informational in nature and are not legal or tax advice, and the authors and publishers are not engaged in the provision of legal, tax, or any other advice.

Front Cover image by 100Covers.com
Book Design by 100Covers.com

Printed by Grab Your Slice, LLC in the United States of America.

First printing edition 2022.

Interior Design by FormattedBooks.com

TABLE OF CONTENTS

FOREWORD

Doug Nordman, co-author (with his daughter
Carol Pittner) of *Raising Your Money-Savvy Family
for Next Generation Financial Independence*

I've known Monica for over five years. When she first contacted me, she was starting her personal finance blog. She wrote "This blog is something for me... to give back... and show from my own life that the little choices one makes in life can have big impacts down the road."

At first, neither of us expected that her choices would lead to this book. Yet with each new blog post, she gradually realized that she had compelling stories and advice to share with her audience.

Everyone takes a different road to their financial independence, and Monica has blazed her own trail. When her consumerism lifestyle ended in debt, divorce, and unemployment, she began the single parent's journey to find work and pay off her credit cards. She went on to build wealth while raising her family.

Whether you're struggling with your finances or growing your family, Monica has figured out the path to success. She shows you how to pay down your debt and improve your credit score to buy your first investment rental property. You'll learn how to assess a building's condition and analyze its cash flow. You'll network (both in your local community and online) to build your team of mentors, real-estate professionals, and financial advisors. You'll figure out your work/life balance among your career, your family, and your properties.

While you're building your real estate investments, you'll also grow your wealth for financial independence.

Monica wrote this book to help other single parents build on her success. She made plenty of mistakes, and she shares them all. She explains how to develop your own processes to succeed in both building your wealth and your new life. She enjoys watching her kids grow up and launch from the nest. Her career has been challenging and fulfilling, yet she's eagerly beginning her financial freedom. We've spent hours discussing her plans and how she'll figure out what she wants to do all day.

She might still feel a little nervous about finally reaching her goals—but she knows how she wants to take her first steps on her new path.

Her journey (and its struggles) has made her stronger. You'll find your own strength from her experiences, and she'll help you build your wealth.

Start making your life choices today.

DEDICATION

To *my kids*. Without them, I would never have found the strength to be the best version of me.

To *my significant other and life partner*, who accepts me as I am, flaws and all.

To *my mom*, the financial magician, who could take $1.00 and make it stretch to $4.00.

To *my friends and family* who have supported me every step of the way on this crazy journey. You know who you are!

I love you guys!!

INTRODUCTION

I'm better than I used to be. Better than I was yesterday.
But hopefully not as good as I'm going to be tomorrow.
Marianne Williamson

It was a crisp Sunday evening, the kids (preschool and kindergarten age) were at their dads for the weekend. The house was quiet and still. I sat in the living room with my laptop and my phone. I knew these two days would come. What I didn't count on was that both happened on the same day.

Friday was the last day at my temp job, and I needed to file for unemployment. Ironically, this was also the weekend I was eligible to file for my divorce (in North Carolina, married couples must live separately for one year before filing).

Luckily, I could file for both online, which was perfect because I was emotionally spent. With no family in the area, I called my closest friend to stay on the phone with me while I handled the paperwork.

I was scared, overwhelmed, beaten down, and tired. Once the divorce and unemployment paperwork were filed, I set out on an adventure that, in my wildest dreams, I could never have imagined.

Wild because this is where I started. Below is a snapshot of my net worth at that moment and where my story began:

DEBT: $ 257,000

- $ 122,000 House Mortgage
- $ 135,000 "Other" Debt

ASSETS (Cash - Liquid): $ 104,050

- $ 20,000 non-retirement accounts
- $ 7,000 savings account
- $ 77,050 retirement account
- $ 4,500 529's

ASSETS (Property – Non-Liquid): $ 325,000

- $ 325,000 House (Purchase Price)

That Sunday night, after filing all the correct paperwork and saying good night to my friend, I stared at my net worth and all the debt that was now squarely on my shoulders alone. It was devastating. *$257,000!!??!!* "That's a quarter of a million dollars!!," I thought. How did things get so bad so fast? I was never going to get my share of the "American dream" with all that debt. I was never going to get my own slice of the pie if I didn't make some life changes.

That night, I made a promise to myself and my kids. I would never allow us to be in such a vulnerable position again. My priority was to get back our security and achieve financial independence. In my mind I thought a net worth of $1,000,000 would give me that.

From that moment on, I focused and inched my way toward this arbitrary goal and was able to grow my net worth substantially. Did I hit that million-dollar net worth? Here's my story.

HOW THIS BOOK IS ORGANIZED

I like pie. Do you? What I like about pie, other than the taste, is how versatile it is. There are so many fillings to choose from and yet the basic pie crust generally remains the same with flour, butter, salt, and sugar. They must be added in just the right way for a flaky crust that can hold the densest of fillings without falling apart. Picking a crust and filling combination is kind of up to you. What is your favorite filling? Are you a traditional apple pie enthusiast? Will you make an elaborate lattice top crust or leave it open so you can dig right in? Creating your own path to Financial Independence (FI) is, in a lot of ways, like making a pie. Here you will have all the tools (and ingredients) you need to make your very own pie, of financial independence that is. It's a FI Pie.

To demonstrate how to make a FI Pie, this book is organized by phases. Each phase starts with my own recipe then outlines steps to make your own custom financial independence pie. There are six phases to move through.

Phase Zero: No Pie. Mindless spending and there is little to no pie, i.e., savings or investments of any type.

Phase One: Take Inventory and Build a Crust. Define the financial starting point and take the first steps towards building a solid foundation to achieving financial independence.

Phase Two: Tools and Directions. Understand what tools are available in the toolbox and begin experimenting with fillings, i.e., different ways to build income streams.

Phase Three: FI Pie Fillings. Customize the recipe and build out the financial independence pie that supports the perfect-for-me lifestyle.

Phase Four: Slice Size. While the FI Pie is *"in the oven"*, begin planning out how much monthly income is needed for Financial Independence to support the perfect-to-me lifestyle and how much the income streams (filling) will yield monthly.

Phase Five: Serve and Enjoy. Serve and enjoy a big fat FI slice with confidence and joy. That could mean quitting your day job, or not. The choice is yours.

As you read this book, you will find that my FI journey was not a straight line. In other words, I experimented with many fillings that did not work out before creating the recipe that supported the lifestyle I wanted. In many ways, this is how a master baker learns. There were many setbacks. But with persistence and commitment I was able to achieve my own definition of financial independence. I wrote this book so that while you are on your own journey to financial independence you won't be discouraged at going backwards for a little while before going forward again.

Here are some truths to keep in mind while perfecting your FI Pie recipe:

1) **No one-size-fits-all:** Each person has their own favorite pie. In the same way, your definition of financial independence is unique to your lifestyle. What works for one person may be completely different for another. There is no one-size-fits-all recipe.

2) **It takes as long as you need it to:** For some, baking skills come naturally, making the process of producing delicious pies

stress-free. But the experience is not the same for everyone. It's because of this that there is no set amount of time to go through a phase. Each person's starting point, circumstances, and grit will play a role in how long each phase takes.

3) **There is no straight line to success:** You may find yourself advancing to the next phase only to take a step back and revisit a previous phase before ultimately moving forward. This is all part of the journey.

4) **You are unique** and so are your tastes. Be truthful and honest with yourself. Raise your standards. The more you can do, the more amazing the journey is. What got you to this point will not get you to the next level. Be all you – strong and brave.

5) **Celebrate the wins.** You worked hard to take steps and move forward, small, or big. Take a moment to acknowledge your courage and perseverance. Treat yourself.

Customizing your FI Pie recipe takes time and patience. But I promise you, once you settle on the right-for-you recipe, with enough grit and perseverance, nothing can stop you from making it and grabbing your slice of financial independence.

PHASE ZERO:
PIE? WHAT PIE?
EAT EVERYTHING!!

Though being financially independent can be defined differently for everyone, it generally means not being dependent on a job or anyone else to meet your expenses and maintain your chosen lifestyle.

Rebecca Lake, SmartAsset.com

LIFE BEFORE FINANCIAL INDEPENDENCE

I am a first-generation citizen and grew up in the United States. I point it out because it was a heavy influence growing up. My parents came to this country, without speaking English, without money, without family. They became US citizens seven years after emigrating here.

What they lacked in language, cash, and support, they more than made up for in courage, grit, and perseverance. Something they passed on to me just by watching. As a young adult, I didn't do a lot of listening to my parents' advice and wisdom. I thought I had it all figured out. I would think, "what do they know? They didn't grow up here. It's a completely different experience."

Part of that is true; growing up in the United States is different from, well, most other countries. My parents both grew up poor, and in difficult families. But they were disciplined in managing their finances and masters at stretching dollars. They were, what is considered now, *old school*.

That is to say, they didn't believe in credit cards or debt. They paid in cash whenever possible. Their rainy-day fund was kept in the bottom drawer of my mom's nightstand. They ran their own business and worked hard, long days. I remember, as a kid, going to the shop after school until their workday was over.

3

Young Life

By the time I was 12 years old, my dad would have me sit with him to pay the stack of bills that came in the mail. He would write checks and I would stuff envelopes. Occasionally, he would have me read a letter or two from customers or other businesses and write the replies.

Neither of my parents completed elementary school. They had to go to work to help support their respective families. Both grew up in the same small town with no prospects for opportunity. Which is why, when my dad was offered a job in the United States, he jumped at the chance. After marrying my mom, he came to the United States first to establish himself. A year later my mom followed. She had never lived anywhere else but her small town. Everything she ever knew and all the people she loved were back home. I can only imagine how hard it was for her to leave everything familiar behind.

It's hard to wrap my head around what they went through to have a better life for themselves and their children. Growing up, at times, I may have seemed ungrateful and maybe even a little spoiled. Looking back, I would agree.

Mom and I butted heads quite a bit as I grew up, like most mother-teenage daughter relationships. She loved me and was enormously proud of my accomplishments, as if they were her own. And at times she was frustrated because she sacrificed her own life, her youth, so I could have a better life. I had my whole life ahead of me and opportunities were thrown at my feet compared to what my parents had available to them. It took many years to fully appreciate what they tried to get me to understand all along.

My dad was a man of few words when it came to us kids. He was more the type of parent that would just give you a *look*. The *look* that many kids can relate to. The *look* where if you messed up, you knew it was not going to be pretty when you got home. His famous catch phrase was, "what you need is a kick in the ass." That was his version of "straighten up and do better." And it wasn't just to us kids, he would say that about customers, politicians, and pretty much anyone that was getting on his nerves. If he were around today, he would be trending with *#kickintheass*.

First Job

I got my first job at the age of fifteen. Back then I needed a letter, signed by a parent, making it okay to get a job. With an already written letter in hand, I handed it to my dad and asked him for his signature. He thought this was a terrible idea and asked, "why do you want to get a job now? Wait another year, enjoy the summer." But I was headstrong and had to do things my way. If he said left, I would go right. I told him I wanted to, "make my own money, spend it the way I wanted, and without asking permission." Reluctantly, he signed the letter.

#kickintheass

When it came to managing my new income stream, I really had no idea what I was doing with my earned money. My dad mentioned once or twice the 50-30-20 rule (50% towards basic living needs, 30% towards wants, 20% towards savings). I watched my mom magically stretch dollars like a financial magician.

These concepts sounded good, but I did not think I would need them, and if I did, I wasn't really sure *how* to apply it in my life. Instead, I wasted money, eating out all the time and buying clothes just because I could, generally spending my whole paycheck. I was having fun and enjoying the freedom that money brings.

After graduating high school, my dad tried to convince me to get a job at a bank. Why? Because I could work my way up and eventually "make a million dollars with job security" and "if I didn't want to do that, that was fine... just fine." Of course, as a teenager, I already "knew everything" and didn't take his advice.

I was the first in my family to graduate college and eventually took a job as a Business Analyst.

That Costa Rica Trip

When I was 23 years old, a friend of mine invited me to take a week-long girls' trip to Costa Rica. Even though I had been working since I was 15, I literally had no money, spending as quickly as I earned it. There was only one response I could give: "Of course I want to go!!!"

I could go because I lived at home. The only real expense I had was my car and lifestyle. In an immigrant family, living with your parents is normal. The kids move out when they marry, most of the time, but sometimes the spouse moves in. It's not uncommon to have up to three generations living under one roof.

With the girls' trip on the horizon, I applied for my first credit card. My parents were anti-credit card, anti-debt. I still managed to get my hands on one and paid it off at the end of each month, most of the time. I charged the entire trip; airline tickets, hotel, food, activities, and excursions without a single thought to how much all of this was going to cost. No budget. It didn't matter, I rationalized to myself. The experience was worth it. I had a job and a college degree. My salary had nowhere to go but up.

Then the bill came. It was my *#kickintheass* and was the most debt I had ever been in. To be completely honest, it stressed me out a little. Up until this point, I spent up to my whole paycheck. Any overspending I did was rare and minimal. But this time was different. I had to really think about how I was going to pay it off.

It took a few months but when I made the last payment, I announced, happily and loudly, to my coworkers, "I am worth nothing!" I explained that I paid off my credit card debt with the remaining dollars in my savings account. No rainy-day funds. No investments. And now, no more debt.

I'll never forget the looks on their faces as they stared at me, then looked at each other with a little smile before turning back to me. They never said a word, just let me have my moment. In my mind,

I thought, "they must think I am so clever! I am, after all, living the American dream!"

What I have come to understand is when my parents left their home and came to this country, it was not to go into debt by consuming mindlessly. They came with an appreciation for all the opportunity the United States has to offer and to build a life they could only have dreamed of if they stayed back home. They became U.S. citizens and were proud of it.

Now as an adult, I look back and sometimes wonder how bad would things need to be to make the decision to move to a different country, not knowing the language, with no money, or support structure? As I got older, my mom shared some of her childhood with me. I suddenly realized how fortunate I truly am. And how I was so blind to these lessons when I was young and carefree.

Moving Out

At 25, I moved to California and lived on my own for six months before moving in with my boyfriend. I had a full-time job, $2,000 in savings and a paid off car. My boyfriend, on the other hand, had a full-time job, $0 in savings, $2,000 in credit card debt, and recently had been in a car accident where his car was totaled. Worse, he allowed his car insurance to lapse. I paid off his debt and we shared my car.

This was the first of many, *many* mistakes. When I look back, I shake my head and wonder what in the world was I thinking? While we lived together, I managed the monthly bills, not because we discussed it but because it just defaulted to me.

After we were married, I deferred the responsibility to him. I assumed he would handle the finances the same way I did. We never talked about money. So long as the lights turned on, I thought we were good. I assumed we were on the same page.

Then one day, I picked up the mail and opened our credit card bill. I was shocked and angry that within two months it was over

$5,000!!!! We were behind on utility bills as well. When I confronted him, he was genuinely confused at my anger. He said, "everyone paid the minimum on their credit card statement" and that "it was normal to carry debt." Apparently, he was living his American dream. In my mind, he needed a #kickintheass.

I couldn't live that way and took back the responsibility of paying the bills, which was fine with him since he didn't want to do it in the first place. After a few months, all the bills were caught up and we had no debt. I was so happy and proud, just like my Costa Rica trip years back. I couldn't wait to share the news with my husband. All excited, I told him we were finally debt free and was ready to celebrate. But he was unimpressed and didn't understand what the big deal was.

Even after this, we still did not talk about money or expectations. No surprise, things only got worse. I had boundaries on my spending, he did not. If he wanted something, he would buy it, and most of the time not even tell me. He never worried about how something would be paid, that was my problem. It never bothered him to carry debt. To him, it was normal. He would rationalize his spending by saying he didn't get things growing up. Buying things brought him happiness, even if the feeling of being happy was fleeting.

Then after a few years of marriage and renting he wanted to buy a house. I told him we needed to save up as we didn't have the money. This somewhat motivated him. Eventually, we bought a small 1,400 sq foot, 3-bed, 2-bath ranch style house for $255,000, roughly $182.14 per square foot in California. A few years later, we had two kids. Family life kept me busy.

One day, my husband came to me with a serious look on his face and said we needed to talk. He asked me to sit down and got right to the point. He confessed he had opened a credit card in his own name and now owed thousands of dollars. I don't remember the exact amount. He realized he had no choice but to tell me because I handled the family finances. When I asked him what he spent it on, he wouldn't tell me. All he said was we had to pay it off because the credit card company threatened to put a lien on our house if we didn't.

#kickintheass

This was another mistake on my part, to continue to blindly trust. He apologized and promised things would change and get better.

A New Start

One weekend, at a dinner party, some friends of ours shared that they were relocating to North Carolina. They talked about its family friendly lifestyle, lower cost of living, and reasonable housing prices. The more they talked, the more excited we got. It all sounded great, especially the cost of living. We started to talk about the possibility of relocating too and decided the only way to know if this was right for us was to go out there ourselves. We packed up the kids and spent a week looking at potential homes and seeing the sights. On the last day of our trip, we decided to put a bid on a house, then got on the plane and flew back to California. By the time we got home the offer was accepted. We now owned two homes, one on each coast. And just like that, we quit our jobs, packed our bags, and put our house on the market.

We sold our ranch house for $800,000, roughly $571.43 per square foot. If you are doing the quick math, we made a tidy profit of over $500,000. It was like winning the lottery!

We moved to North Carolina and moved into our a 3,000 sq foot, 4-bed house for $325,000 ($108.33 per square foot) and decided to *not* pay in full. We ended up taking a 30-year fixed loan at 5.25% which cost us about $745 per month, not including property taxes and insurance which was an additional $380 per month.

He was lucky and found a job six months after moving and I stayed home with the kids for the first year. The first three years, we were spending like crazy. Between the sale of our California house and the overall lower cost of living in North Carolina, we suddenly had actual money. I loosely kept track of the spending but didn't really pay attention to our dwindling savings account. In that time, we did a lot of damage with one poor financial decision after another.

How much damage? Well, to recap, we sold our home at a huge profit, moved, and bought a house that was twice as big, opened a Home Equity Line of Credit (HELOC), and began spending. What did we spend on? Below are the highlights:

- Upgraded the kitchen with custom cabinets, professional appliances, and added dual ovens.
- Upgraded the eat-in breakfast nook and butler's pantry.
- Added a dry wine bar (with glass door mini fridge).
- Installed a new roof (really, the only justifiable expense).
- Added custom built-in bookcases in the informal living room.
- Added a pocket door between the formal and informal living rooms which required foundational reinforcement for the load bearing wall.
- Built a large screened-in porch with tile floor on the upper deck and repaired the attached uncovered lower deck.
- Completely remodeled the back yard with not one but two retaining walls, added a limestone path covered with a custom-built pergola that led to a large limestone patio area, and added a playground.
- Upgraded the front yard with a third retaining wall and large open stone patio with, of course, a beautiful custom pattern in the middle.
- Let us not forget furnishing this new home that was twice the size of our previous home.
- Purchased a two bed/ two bath townhouse with the HELOC for $105,000 and furnished it (for when the family and friends came to visit, naturally.)

- Purchased a used Volvo convertible.
- All this while keeping our standard of living: eating out, entertaining, traveling, etc.

Our spending was so out of control, we ended up borrowing money from family to help with the expenses! *Ridiculous,* I know. The one thing we did right was pay them back.

A few years later, we separated. He moved into the townhouse, and I stayed in the home with the kids for stability. I tell you all of this, my litany of mistakes, because I'm guessing you have made a few of your own. Maybe not as big as mine, maybe you think yours are bigger. Regardless, you know how this book ends, I found financial independence. I will go over the how and my mistakes on that path as well. Just know, if you are here, if you are just filing for divorce or find yourself under a pile of debt: I was there too. And I got out of it. Many people do. You've picked up this book, you've decided to try to fix it. You've already taken your first step.

Sometimes, before we can move forward, we need to look back. Not in a dwell and feel-sorry-for-yourself kind of way, but in more of an understand-where-the-mistakes-happened-and-learn-from-them way and then move forward. I believe, if we don't learn from past mistakes, we are bound to repeat them. One thing was for sure, I didn't want to do that. Moving forward, my plan was to build a life worth reliving.

I spent time reflecting on all my decisions up to that point and how my parents handled their money and the full life they lived with friends, even going back home every few years to visit family.

I asked myself, what does a life worth reliving look like? The answer was simple. *To have enough passive income to pay the bills and take a vacation or two without ever relying on a paycheck.* Having this overarching goal has been my North Star, my guiding light, when I was unclear which direction to go.

---

*What does a life worth reliving look like for you? Take
a moment and reflect on your own life. How important
is financial independence (FI)? What do you want
to achieve? What are you willing to do to get there?*

Below are two reflections I would often revisit to keep me motivated in my journey to financial independence:

- First, I needed to define my why, as in, why is financial independence important. I wrote it down, kept it visible, and read it every morning.
- Second, I needed to write goals that supported my why and would be updated with each step forward. This was especially important as I discovered and refined my personal FI Pie recipe.

Reading these two things every morning kept me driven, especially when some FI Pie recipes didn't work. Looking back, the mistakes I made were invaluable lessons that made me stronger in future decisions.

What I know is, there is no one recipe that fits all tastes, but instead one FI Pie recipe that is perfect for each of us.

My hope is through sharing my own journey and the phases I went through, that you too will discover your perfect FI Pie recipe. Take some time and be open and honest with yourself throughout the phases. Keep learning and discovering. Know that creating your perfect FI Pie recipe takes time and multiple iterations. You may not know your financial independence recipe starting out but going through the phases will get you there. Most importantly, remember to celebrate the wins.

GOAL SETTING

*Your most important work is always ahead
of you, never behind you.*
Stephen Covey, *The 7 Habits of Highly Effective People*

I had come to learn about S.M.A.R.T. goals soon after I started my journey to financial independence. S.M.A.R.T. stands for *Specific, Measurable, Assignable, Relevant,* and *Time-based.*

Once I understood *how* to write a goal, I moved on to my next hurdle – fear.

I suddenly felt a ton of pressure to be better. In my past attempts to write goals, they were written all wrong and half the time I would forget I even wrote them. So, if I failed, there were many rational reasons why I didn't reach them. But with S.M.A.R.T. goals, those excuses were taken away.

"Do I really want to do this?" I thought to myself. "Am I capable? Smart enough?" (pun intended). Up until that point, I realized I had been floating through life, not really paying attention. I was "eating everything." It didn't matter if the pie was good, bad, or even past its expiration date. But now, the blinders were about to come off and it was terrifying.

Using the S.M.A.R.T. method of goal writing, I started small, listing things that needed to get done but were not critical. The truth was, I had no idea what I was capable of. The first order of business was to establish my baseline. I was shocked at the results.

Not only did I achieve all the goals I gave myself an entire year to complete, but I got them all done in the first three months! Suddenly I found myself having to come up with more goals. I wrote up some more that had been in the back of my mind and achieved all of those in the next few months.

Basically, I had to do the goal setting exercise three times that first year. I was shocked and elated. It was as if I discovered a superpower, *my* superpower. Courage overtook my fear. It felt so good.

The second year of using S.M.A.R.T. goals, I made a list that was slightly intimidating AND given how well I did the previous year, I made a separate list of stretch goals (goals that would require a little more sweat and effort to achieve) should I get done early again. This time I was prepared. And you know what? I completed my original list after six months and started pulling from my stretch goal list.

It doesn't matter when you start,
so long as you DO start.

It was such a rush and ego boost to look back at my list of goals that now turned into accomplishments. Over the next few years, goals evolved and eventually were broken up into categories ranging from personal and family, to all things financial independence, as well as house and travel goals. Each category had no more than five goals, each goal ranked from small to large.

Breaking up my goals by category gave me a bird's eye view of my progress and where I focused my energy. Over the years, it became a habit to review my goals every morning and I adjusted as the year progressed. This method forced me to raise my standards through courage and perseverance.

It may all sound demanding or even monotonous, but in truth it never was. My goals were just that, things I wanted to do that were important to me. By raising my standards, I put my needs first. It was empowering.

Over time, my goal setting evolved to fold in long-term goals. My buckets were defined as short-term (one year or less), medium-term (one to five years) and long-term (greater than five years).

Once medium- and long-term goals were defined, I would work my way backwards, breaking them down into smaller goals or support goals. This would serve as a map of how I would achieve each medium- and long-term goal. I would keep my goal sheet someplace where I could read it every day and keep it updated. The medium- and long-term goals would get refined as progress was made and new information came in.

This is how I set goals today. It took me many years and many iterations to get to this format. But I wanted to share it with you up front so you could have a better starting point. If you are interested, go to **GrabYourSlice.com** and sign up to receive freebies like the Goal Setting Template.

Now it's your turn to dream big and be bold. Nothing is off the table. Refine your goals as you learn more about yourself and the opportunities around you. Goal setting is a process that gets updated and refined as you and your lifestyle evolve.

THE FI KITCHEN RULES

The last thing I want to share in this chapter is a list of basic FI kitchen rules. These are truths I learned along the way, but it would have been helpful to really understand them before I started out. You see, I didn't learn about Financial Independence (FI) or the FIRE movement until Year Eight of my journey and everything was turned on its head. Where it makes sense, I share some of those concepts earlier to put you in a better position. For the first eight years of my journey, I learned on my own and my only goal was to never rely on a paycheck, but for you, dear reader, it can be so much more.

1) This is **not a get rich quick plan**. No winning lottery numbers here. But, if you follow the steps, then depending on your starting point, commitment, and grit, financial independence can be achieved in less than the traditional 40, 50, or even 60 years and can be more along the lines of 10, 15 or even 20 years.

2) **Keep an open mind**. Getting financially fit is a lot like getting healthy. It's one thing to go on a diet to lose weight, but it's an entirely different matter to lose weight and want to keep it off. This is more of a *lifestyle change*. A lifestyle that is not only better for you but will support the life you dream of with more energy and clarity. Who wouldn't want that?

3) Just like going on a diet, the chances of success increase when you **have a partner and a plan**. This is your personal plan. Having an accountability partner who can also act as a sounding board is invaluable but not required. A Financial Coach can also serve in this role when you get started.

4) **There is no straight-line to financial independence**. There will be big wins and some losses. The important thing to remember is that setbacks will happen, but it's how you choose to handle them that will set the tone for your journey. Focus on the wins, learn from the losses, and remember to celebrate achievements along the way.

5) **Each person's FI Pie recipe is perfect for them**. One may have a high-risk tolerance and go all in with stocks while another is conservative with a large rainy-day fund. What is important to remember is to *know yourself*, your risk tolerance, and what you need in hand to cover your own lifestyle and goals. Knowing this is the first step.

6) **Refer to the foundational steps defined above throughout your journey**. About once a year, I would review my own recipe and adjust as it made sense. I would ask myself, was I getting any closer to creating my perfect FI Pie recipe? Did this year's steps get me closer to my why? Does this plan still make me happy? Does this lifestyle and spending reflect who I truly am?

We are ever evolving and growing. What mattered five years ago may no longer be the case. Keep an open mind. Pace yourself.

EXERCISE: DEFINE YOUR WHY AND WHY NOW?

The WHY is the purpose, cause, or belief
that drives every one of us.
Simon Sinek, *Start With Why*

There is no time like the present. Defining your *why* serves as the overarching goal under which everything else is measured. It serves as a guiding light when you are either at a fork in your journey or are losing steam to move forward. Your *why* provides inspiration when you think you don't have the strength to move forward. It can also be the encouragement that picks you up when you are knocked down. Here are some things to keep in mind when writing your *why* statement.

Personal and Unique. Your *why* is personal and unique to your life. Sure, most want the same thing: more time with family and friends, to work less (or not at all), or to take more vacations. But *your* personal why goes deeper than that. The *why* statement will remind you specifically why you started on this journey to begin with. When you think about your future life, what does it look like?

Propelling Forward. Your *why* is what is propelling you forward to something better, more suited to you and the lifestyle you want. It should get you excited. This is different from moving away from something. Moving away is only half a journey and doesn't answer the question of what's next.

Be Specific. The more specific the better. Are you committing to the FI journey at this point in your life to make a better life for your kids, for yourself, or maybe both? Whatever your definition of financial independence is, it should be honest and reflect your true self.

Remember, there is no right or wrong but only what matters to you and your lifestyle.

Take some time to reflect on your life, what has mattered, what hasn't, and what you want more (and less) of. Think about what your perfect lifestyle would look like. Getting your finances in order will assist in building and supporting that future lifestyle you imagine.

Write out the definition of your perfect lifestyle. Remember to put it somewhere you can read it every day. Here are some questions to ask yourself and get inspired. Think big. Be bold. Nothing is off the table.

- Why are you on this journey?
- What does a life worth re-living look like for you?
- What makes you happy?
- What is your definition of financial independence?
- Why do you want financial independence in your life?
- What mistakes have you made and what have you learned from them?

Exercise: Set Your Own S.M.A.R.T. Goals

Begin by defining three categories that are important in your life and could use some focus. Some examples are, Personal, Professional, Travel, Religious, Family, Financial, and Home.

For Beginners: If you are new to S.M.A.R.T. goal setting, begin with smaller goals for the next six months. Keep the list where you can read it every day for inspiration and guidance. This is an opportunity to baseline yourself and know what you are truly capable of.

For More Experienced Goal-Setters: If you are a natural goal-setter but don't look past the next 12 months, your homework is to think about what you want your life to look like and the things you want to achieve five years from now. Use the following buckets to guide you:

- <u>Short-Term</u>: one year or less
- <u>Medium-Term</u>: one to five years
- <u>Long-Term</u>: greater than five years

For medium- and long-term goals, work backwards from when the goal should be completed, continually refine, and make updates as you take steps towards achieving the goal and as opportunities present themselves. Life is rarely lived in a straight line.

Goal Categories: Grouping goals into buckets is a great way to see where your attention is focused as things are checked off. For example, let's say you set three goals each for Health, Career, and Family categories. Midyear, you look at your goal list and are proud to see that two of the three goals are completed in Career and Family, but none in Health. That tells you that Family and Career are important. But it also shows that focus needs to be shifted to Health goals. Grouping goals into categories along with short-, medium-, and long-term goals gives an added dimension that is invaluable.

Lastly, make sure to put a date at the top of the list of goals as a starting point. This will make the S.M.A.R.T. goal list more tangible.

PHASE **ONE**:
TAKE INVENTORY AND
THE PERFECT FI CRUST

You can't really know where you are going until
you know where you have been.

Maya Angelou

YEAR ONE: PANTRY INVENTORY (DEFINE MY STARTING POINT)

If I had to pick one song to summarize Year One on this journey, it would be, I Dreamed a Dream from Les Misérables. Like most people, when I got married, it wasn't with the idea of divorcing years later. While this was a difficult decision it was, without question, the right decision for all of us.

Starting the year newly separated, the dust had settled, and the reality was a tough pill to swallow. I spent much of this year going through the stages of grief that often come with the end of a long relationship, finally accepting that all our decisions brought us to this point. More importantly, moving forward, I understood that I had the power to change my story and that what happened next was up to me.

I had lived on my own for a total of six months up to that point. I went from living at home with my parents to living with my husband with very little independent time in between. Now separated, the stakes were higher with a house, mortgage, debt, and two little kids hanging in the balance of every decision made moving forward. I'm not going to lie; it was simultaneously scary and freeing.

Armed with my definition of financial independence, my why, and some high-level goals, it was time to get started.

I focused on three areas:

1) Financial: Record spending and income consistently.
2) Professional: Obtain a new job.
3) Home: Take inventory of what I did have.

You know that moment in the day when all you want is something sweet? And, how a slice of your favorite homemade pie would taste so good right about now? But then you realize that not only do you not have anything sweet, but you are not even sure if you have all the ingredients to make something? That you are not even sure where all the tools are? Then that feeling of disappointment, wondering, when did things get so disorganized? That was the starting point I found myself in with my FI Pie.

I didn't let any of this deter me and was determined to focus on the things I could control.

My First (Real) Household Budget

I had budgeted in the past with no success. To do it again, I thought, would be an exercise in insanity (i.e., doing the same thing over and over and expecting a different result). This time I set out to do budgeting differently. "There are so many success stories out there," I thought, "what am I doing wrong?" Turns out, I was doing everything wrong. No wonder it never worked.

My first mistake was creating a budget based on what I *thought* I was spending instead of what I was *actually* spending. I would pull monthly spending amounts out of my head for a given category. Doing it this way would leave me with a feeling of frustration and scarcity. Sound familiar? Other big mistakes included:

Not recording spending and income consistently. Starting out, a
friend of mine offered to sit with me for the first three or four

months and review my cash flow. I quickly realized that I had a lot of spending happening that was not recorded at all or not categorized in a way that gave me a better understanding of the household cashflow.

Not budgeting for annual expenses. Not taking annual expenses, like property taxes, into account every month made my budget lopsided. Basically, I would wait until the end of the year then scramble to figure out where the money would come from.

Not budgeting for fun like vacations. Not setting aside funds every month to pay for such trips would leave me scrambling to cover the expense.

Not understanding that budgeting is very flexible. It never occurred to me that budgeting is actually quite flexible. If I overspent in one category, I could either a) reel in spending in other categories to make up the difference for the month or I could b) reel in spending the next month to make up the difference for the year.

In other words, to know where I could be flexible with my cash flow, I had to be consistent with recording every expense and all income. Understanding my true spending gave me new insights and confidence when I did spend. I went back to basics, if I didn't have the money in hand, I wouldn't buy it.

Once I had a few months of cash flow data, I found some interesting trends. I was surprised at how much I spent on groceries, dining out, and some discretionary items. The other surprise was some of the newly added categories to reflect spending that was not being captured, like, out of pocket medical expenses, annual memberships, and home repairs.

Halfway through the year, I would compare actual spending with what was planned and adjusted the budget to reflect true spending more accurately. Doing this gave me a sense of how to handle the rest of the year, identifying areas where I could be more conservative or liberal.

Just like goal setting, budgeting also went through many iterations and evolutions over several years before getting to where I am today. As I learned more about spending and saving habits, I added in the following steps:

- **Pay Myself First – Rainy-Day Account**: Leveraging direct deposit, I made sure that a small percentage of my paycheck went to my rainy-day fund. This one move ensured that I paid myself first before I started spending.
- **Pay Myself First – Retirement Account**: Again, leveraging direct deposit from my paycheck, I made sure to put a small percentage into my 401(k).
- **Gave Myself a Raise**: At the end of each month, I analyzed the previous month's spend and trimmed in areas I could. Any extra money found went to my rainy-day fund.
- **Extra Money**: Since I made so little, I got a tax refund most years. This additional money went to my rainy-day fund. I did everything I could to steer clear of lifestyle creep (spending more with each bump in pay or bonus). Moving this extra money directly to my rainy-day fund ensured that it would not be spent on frivolous things but bookmarked for use when in between jobs.
- **Debt Repayment**: I haven't forgotten about the $135,000 debt sitting in the HELOC (Home Equity Line of Credit.) Since the near future was uncertain, I made the decision to pay the minimum and on time, until I was on more stable ground. Doing this kept my credit score stable.

With cash flow data in hand and a budget based on actual income and spending in place, the remaining income was direct deposited in my checking account and spent with confidence. I knew if I stuck to my budget, I wouldn't be overdrawn. More importantly, when an emergency came up, I was prepared because I had rainy-day money, so I didn't worry about going further into debt.

Over time, the notion of *paying myself first* became a mantra. No more excuses. It was a very conscious decision to prioritize myself. Whatever income I made had to stretch and that stretch included paying myself first with each paycheck.

The Job Front

The best way to find your next job is while you currently have a job, or so the saying goes. That lesson became very clear. My truth was I had a temp job that was going to end at the end of the year, if not sooner. My workload was slowly drying up. The writing was on the wall.

The entire year I spent time trying everything I could to find alternate employment. I networked with friends and coworkers, putting the word out that I was available for a new opportunity. I updated my resume with the help of another friend who was much better at writing resumes than I was. I asked co-workers to write a recommendation on my LinkedIn profile to show I was a quality employee who was easy to work with and wasn't afraid of hard work. But I also had restrictions that kept me from taking just any job. After all, I was now a single parent with two young children. Any job I applied for had to fit the following minimum criteria:

1) Less than a 30-minute commute
2) Standard business hours of Monday through Friday 9:00 a.m. to 5:00 p.m.
3) No overtime or travel required
4) No night/weekend work (First shift only)
5) Paid enough to cover expenses and a little extra

Because of these criteria, the kids attended before and after school care which was offered at the elementary school. It would make for long school days, and I would feel super guilty about it. But what choice did I have?

There were so few jobs to apply for and my criteria made it near impossible to find employment. Worse, for every job posted, there were literally dozens of applicants. It was an employer's market. Recruiters were literally tossing out resumes simply because they didn't like the font or format used. With so many resumes to choose from, recruiters could afford to be extra picky.

My contract job ended a month before the holidays. With no job prospects in sight, I spent the rest of the year on unemployment.

Inventory the Pantry

By the end of the fourth quarter, my divorce was finalized. I had time on my hands and a rainy-day fund to float us for a little while. I turned some financial tasks into a game, challenging myself to spend a little less than the previous month. "Forget about 'the Joneses' next door," I told myself. Besides, there was no way for me to keep up, they literally had a pool and jacuzzi. Even with all the upgrades to our own house, we didn't have that.

With this downtime, I took inventory of what I could control: dining out and entertainment. I reminded myself, this was just a point in time and not forever, though at times, it felt like these tough times were never going to end.

Food was a big expense especially with two kids to feed. Luckily, I enjoyed being in the kitchen and didn't go out to eat a whole lot. Still, we could do better. At the end of each week, I made a menu for the following week. This would ensure I only bought what we needed and wasted almost nothing. What also helped was making a theme for each day. For example:

Mondays: chicken.

Tuesdays: tacos.

Wednesdays: pasta/vegetarian.

Thursdays: soup or stew.

Fridays: fish.

Saturday and Sundays: reserved for leftovers or sandwiches.

When employed, I would do my grocery shopping on a Saturday and food prep for the week on Sunday. Whenever possible I would double recipes and freeze half for a quick weeknight meal.

When unemployed, I would cut down on grocery costs by spending time making more things from scratch. A bag of flour and carton of eggs could make a lot of pasta to last a couple of weeks when stored in the freezer. I clipped coupons and made the most of sale prices and double coupon days at my local grocery store.

My mom called me one day to share how she made three dinners with one chicken by using the breasts for one dinner, legs, wings, and thighs for a second, and the carcass to make chicken soup. With a little creativity, there are many ways to stretch food dollars.

The Taste Test Game and Mealtime Rules

To keep meals interesting, the kids and I would play a game called *The Taste Test*. This was my way of exposing them to different foods and in a frugal way. For example, as an afternoon snack, I bought different pear varieties. I washed and sliced each one and put each pear variety on their own plate with a label. With pears on the table, we were ready to start the game.

The kids would try a slice from each plate, and we would talk about how it tasted, what they liked and didn't. Then I would ask which pear was the winner and why. The "winner" pear would be the one I would buy more of. This gave them a say as to what they would eat and there would be less waste. I did this with all kinds of foods.

Another way we kept from wasting food was setting mealtime rules.

Rule #1: Wash your hands.
Rule #2: Try everything.
Rule #3: Clear your plate before asking for more and use "May I have more...".
Rule #4: Use "Please" and "Thank you".
Rule #5: Ask to be excused.
Rule #6: Clear your area and put dishes in kitchen.

The rule that got the most attention was *Try Everything*. The definition of *try* was to take one full bite, chew, and swallow. If they tried to skimp and take a half bite or less, they would get called out and take another *legal* bite.

We would talk about what we liked and didn't. If there was something on their plate they didn't like, they did not have to finish it. No judgement.

There was no misunderstanding of mealtime rules since I wrote them in marker on a large, easel sized piece of paper. There was no getting around them either. What was fun was when friends came over for dinner. The kids would showoff the mealtime rules and explained they applied to everyone, no exceptions. Imagine going to a friend's house for dinner, only to have their kids do the serving and ask you what you thought of each thing on your plate? This made for interesting and fun table conversation. Nothing got past the kids, if they had to eat it, they made sure I did too.

Every so often one or both kids would challenge a rule. I would always hear them out. Sometimes they found a loophole to leverage, which I would allow one time. But after they would go to bed, I would go back to the rules and make an edit to close the loop. That also meant that loophole was closed to everyone no matter what. My point is, food and mealtime can be a great way to open communication with kids while eating at home and it doesn't have to cost a fortune.

Lastly, to ensure mealtime was satisfying for everyone, I made sure to have at least one thing each of the kids would eat. Maybe not love but would eat. This was because I did not make separate meals for the kids from my own, ever. What was on the table was for dinner, no exceptions. There was no going to the refrigerator to make a sandwich because they didn't want to eat what was on the table. I would tell them, "This isn't Burger King. You don't get things your way." Luckily, that almost never happened.

Dining Out Inexpensively

When we did go out to eat it was limited to once a week at most. We only went to restaurants running a special, like, free kid meal with adult meal purchased or $5 off a large pizza. Sometimes I would order one adult meal, split it between the kids and I would eat the kid meal. It was our special treat to celebrate the week's accomplishments. Sometimes, we would meet up with friends at the park and split a pizza. When friends would ask if I wanted to go out for dinner, I would usually decline and invite them over for potluck dinner. On the rare occasion I would go out I would order something small or order a regular meal, eat half, and take the rest to go.

Fun on a Budget

Another common big expense for many, and our house was no exception, was entertainment. I had cut the cable earlier in the year and put a rule in the house of no TV during the week. Honestly, even on the weekends, the kids never noticed. It's amazing how many free things there are to do.

On weekdays, by the time I picked them up from school, the evening routine was clear; come home, put things away, make dinner, do homework, have dinner as a family, talk about our day, clear the table, clean up the kitchen, bath time, story time, bedtime.

On weekends, we could stay home and watch a movie, go to the bookstore, attend free activities around town, meet with friends, and of course, there were chores to get done. We didn't have cable for almost three years, and they never noticed. It just became normal.

Thinking Outside the Box

Since jobs were scarce and I had time on my hands, I thought, "maybe this is the time to start my own business." Nothing was off limits. I was free to forge my own path, and of course, continued to look for a job with stable and predictable income.

Looking into starting my own business gave me a feeling of being in control and leveraging other avenues to make some money.

This was the beginning of thinking about what my FI Pie filling would be made up of. Thinking about what would not only sustain me but I would want to make again and again. This pie filling would be my personal favorite. Sure, I could have gone to the store and bought a can of pie filling, but I realized that that would not be enough to last. I needed to learn to make my own if I was ever going to have a hope of not only paying off my debt but creating a FI Pie that would sustain me for years to come.

These were a few things I came up with:

1) **Grandma Please**: I read an article about a nonprofit organization that hired retired volunteers to receive phone calls from latchkey kids who wanted someone to talk to. After some digging, I found it to be not as successful as the original article made it out to be (i.e., no profit, very time consuming and expensive to get off the ground and maintain).

2) **Community Garden**: What could be better than creating a community garden, a place for people to gather around a common interest? To get this off the ground would require a

fair amount of time and capital. Capital, I did not have. In the end, I decided this was best left to the professionals.

3) **Host Monthly "City Dining" Events**: I came across an article about these al fresco city dining events held all around Europe. The organizer would arrange everything from the guest chef to location and ticket sales. But I didn't know any chefs, and this would require a fair amount of time and capital to get set up. Besides, one bad weather day and I could be out serious cash.

4) **Environmental Consultant (for hospitals)**: Another article I came across was about a self-employed Environmental Consultant who worked with hospitals to find ways to be more environmentally friendly while saving money. I sent him an introduction email, pitching my idea of expanding his consulting business by partnering. After some conversations, we decided to give the partnership a go for any new hospitals signed up in my area. I got right to work making cold calls to hospitals and was successful in setting up several face-to-face meetings. But after a few months and no prospects, we decided to dissolve the partnership.

While all these ideas had merit on some level, I realized I couldn't afford to take on big risk where the payoff could be years in the future. That was the one thing all these businesses had in common; any profit could be up to five years in the making and even then, it wasn't guaranteed. I didn't have the money to float us for that long and build a new business that required capital upfront. In the end, I did not feel comfortable taking on this level of risk, as a single-income household. But I'm glad I thought about them. I evaluated my options and now I can look back with no regrets. I made the right choice at the time for me and my situation.

Taking this time to daydream about what my FI Pie filling would be made of also gave me some insights into my own likes and dislikes.

The most glaring thing was that I didn't know who I was anymore, or what I wanted. It's a common trap parents, especially moms, fall into. I spent so much time running from activity to activity and putting my kids' needs in front of my own that before I knew it, I had lost touch with who I was as an individual. It took me a while to get this sorted, but if you are feeling this now, just know you aren't alone. Whether you are a single mom trying to make ends-meet or a mom with a partner and all the help in the world, we can all get lost in our "mom" identity. The important thing is that we focus on how to find it again.

Dear reader, is there a business you have always wanted to try but never had the time or money to do it? Take some time for yourself and daydream about your own FI Pie filling. Nothing should be off the table. Daydreaming doesn't cost you anything and can be incredibly helpful in knowing what your filling will be made up of. Today, side hustles and small businesses are commonplace and easier than ever to start. The hardest part is narrowing down all the options and picking the one or ones that you love the most. Start experimenting with different fillings and see which ones stick. You may be surprised. To this day, I still scribble ideas of things to try. That is part of the fun in making your own FI Pie! It is customized to your own interests and will support your lifestyle.

FI Pie Crust: Adding Ingredients

Year One was all about clearing the pantry of waste and getting rid of anything that didn't support my FI *why* and initial goals. While all these initial steps were a great start, I soon realized it wasn't enough. To really understand, holistically, what my financial starting point was, I needed to dig deeper than just tracking cash flow, and from that, creating a budget template. I added three more ingredients that ultimately became my FI crust: net worth, credit score, and credit history.

I realized that if I wanted that perfect FI Pie, I needed a crust that could hold any filling and not fall apart. Adding these three ingredients would do just that.

After going through a major life change, I realized that I needed to level set. Pulling my credit score gave me some peace in knowing it wasn't too bad but had some room for improvement. I also pulled my credit history to make sure everything on it was actually mine. Thankfully it was.

Ending that year was like coming out of a fog. There were some major challenges ahead of me, but now armed with actual data, I was able to make informed decisions. As I sat and analyzed where my net worth landed at the end of the year, I reminded myself that this was just a point in time. I knew I had the power to change my story and FI Pie recipe.

Be Resourceful

We all have strengths and weaknesses. My strengths are cooking and mad organization skills. My weakness is resume writing. To get my resume updated, I bartered cooking weeknight meals for a friend who was very good at resume writing. We both came out ahead.

What talents can you leverage or barter with friends? What tools will you uncover in your FI pantry?

Another example was leveraging my time. My kids were young (preschool and kindergarten) when I started out. To make the most of my day, I would set my alarm two hours before the kids would get up so I could get in a workout and shower. My lunch hour would sometimes be used to take care of setting appointments or running an errand or two.

Yes, I was tired, but my drive came from reading my why every morning. It would set the tone for why any of these changes were important and what purpose they served. Was everyday perfect and filled with accomplishments? Absolutely not! But at the end of each year, I could clearly see that progress was being made. Life is not lived in a straight line.

Keep your heels, head, and standards high.
Coco Chanel

Lessons Learned

- Finding Courage and Grit. Living on my own with the kids and surviving, I didn't know I had it in me.
- Taking Responsibility. Life happens to everyone; it's how we react that makes the difference.
- Raising Standards. I was financially careless and reckless, but those actions do not dictate the future. I can change things if I want to.

Year End Summary

I was starting over and on my own. My net worth landed at around $246,550 (that was after subtracting out the $257,000 of debt). Most of that was made up of the value of the house. I had a solid understanding of the debt and how to manage it without negatively impacting my credit score. I reviewed my credit history and found it to be accurate.

With these few ingredients I was able to make a pretty good *first pass* at a FI Pie crust. Every year, I would take the opportunity to refine my FI Pie crust and make small changes. At the end of each year, I would refine my budget template in such a way that would give me more information about my spending. I would also refine my goal setting methods to get the most out of each year.

Making FI Pie crust was not a one-and-done recipe but more of an opportunity to refine it to make it as close to perfect for me and the lifestyle I wanted and deserved.

It wasn't until years later when I discovered the FI community. These ideas and concepts were things I came up with on my own and thinking back on how my parents handled their own money.

To see details, go to **grabyourslice.com/year-one.**

EXERCISE: BUILD YOUR BASIC FI PIE CRUST

Even though I have been on this journey for many years, I am still learning and always come back to these four basic yet critical crust ingredients: Net Worth, Credit History, Credit Score, and Cash Flow. Life is a journey, not a destination. As I learned new things about myself and evaluated opportunities that came along, coming back to these four ingredients always helped to steer me in the right direction. Like any good FI crust recipe, modifications can be made to suit your needs. Lastly, remember to review these key ingredients often.

1) Calculating Net Worth

At its basic definition, net worth is simply *totaling all assets and subtracting all debt (liabilities)*. The purpose of calculating net worth is to give a high-level financial picture. This is different from tracking the day-to-day flow of money. It's important to understand the difference between net worth and cash flow as one without the other is useless. Net worth is high level tracking, where cash flow is day-to-day tracking. These two ingredients go hand in hand.

When writing down all your assets and listing out your debts, here are some things to consider:

Do you include your primary home? Automobiles? Collectibles? And anything else of value? There are arguments for adding and not adding them.

Here are some guidelines:

Be Consistent. The only true rule to calculate net worth is to **be consistent** year over year. If you do decide to make a change to how your net worth is calculated and recorded, remember to go back to previous years and adjust those calculations accordingly. That is the only way to know if your net worth is growing and on track with your goals.

The first time I did this exercise, I was horrified at how little I had. I added things to my asset column like my depreciating-in-value car, my furniture (optimistic garage sale price for all of it), and my clothes (I had too many anyway). These things stayed in my Assets column. When I was ready, these things were removed. Having a consistent net worth formula allowed for a fair comparison year over year.

The one benefit to adding these extra things was it got me to look at my finances through a different lens. It highlighted all the different ways I could make money in addition to a paycheck. For example, garage sales not only put cash in my pocket, but also got rid of things that required maintenance. Second, it forced me to take inventory of what I had. It made me realize I did not need to go shopping for more stuff, everything I truly needed I already had. This realization had me spending less and putting more in my pocket every month, which eventually led to my net worth increasing.

A Point in Time. We all have a starting point, the important thing to remember is it's just a point in time. So, if your net worth is not where you want it to be or maybe you are not as far along as you thought you were, take heart in knowing that you have the power to change things by committing to raising your standards.

Your Turn

1) **Starting Out**: Starting out, it's best to have a bird's eye view of what you have accomplished so far and where you stand. On a sheet of paper or excel spreadsheet, calculate your net worth today. Make a list of assets. Make a list of liabilities (debts). Subtract liabilities from assets. Do this consistently at the end of each year and be consistent in how net worth is calculated. This exercise of tracking progress shows the natural progression of mini slices adding up to one big fat slice of FI. When you hit your goals, remember to treat yourself.

2) **Add an extra ingredient (optional)**: In addition to calculating net worth annually, start tracking cash investments monthly, for a more granular view. In a later chapter, I will explain how cash investments can be turned into one form of passive income. It's simple to do. At the end of each month, record the balance of all cash accounts from checking to cash investment funds, like 401(k), index funds, money market, etc. This will help ensure there are no surprises at the end of the year and will motivate you to stay the course. I have an example you can review at **grabyourslice.com/ cash-investment-tracker-sample..**

2) Track the Flow!

What I know to be true is budgeting, done correctly, is liberating. Before creating a budget, take a step back and record the flow of money coming into the house and going out. I did this for a few months before taking a first pass at creating a new budget.

Taking the time to do this consistently will give you invaluable insights. Monthly spending will typically vary depending on what is going on in your life. Another realization I had was how I could cover overspending in one category by taking dollars from an underutilized category in the same month. For example, I overspent in my grocery category by $30 but then underspent in dining out by $30. This would allow my overall monthly budget to be covered.

But what if I overspent in groceries by $30 and didn't have the money to cover it from a different category in the same month? Then I knew I needed to reel in spending the next month to make up the difference. Maybe that meant going out to eat less or cutting back on other nonessentials. How I did it was my choice. And I had the tools to get me back on track. Understanding this level of flexibility gave me confidence.

The last realization was planning for future expenses. After a while, I was able to start planning for annual expenses like property taxes or insurance. I just made sure to take the one-time expenses, divide by twelve, and that was the amount I would put aside each month. When it came time to pay these big-ticket items, the money was ready and without disrupting my flow.

Over many years, I got the hang of budgeting. Through tracking cash flow, there was no question in my mind that it was a powerful tool. And to think it all started with recording my flow.

The last thing I would like to discuss about cash flow is handling cash. Cash can be a little tricky. Keeping a notepad and pen or recording the spend on your cell phone is great. Replacing the cash with receipts in your wallet is also a good way to do it. Most important is to make sure to enter the expenses in your budget when you get home before the end of the day. Record it while it's still fresh in your mind.

Your Turn: Budget 1.0 – The First Pass

1) Record cash flow for at least two to three months.
2) If you do not want to manually record everything in an Excel spreadsheet, have no fear there are plenty of free tools

out there that can make this part amazingly easy, just search online for "Best Free Budgeting Apps".

3) Once you have the habit of consistently tracking your money, and have about two to three months of data, take a first pass at creating a budget.

4) At the end of the month, compare spending by category to the previous month. Adjust the budget as necessary.

5) Don't worry about getting it perfect. I have no doubt that, just like mine, your budget will go through iterations as you track more of your cash flow and learn more about where your money actually goes.

Rules of Recording Income and Spending

1) **Don't change habits** ... at least not for this first pass. Spend as you normally would. The purpose of this is to understand *how* you use money. I really can't stress this step enough. The reason we feel so discouraged about budgeting is because we don't do it right. Take the time to know your money flow first before going out and getting a budgeting tool to support it.

2) **Be consistent** in using categories. Use a budget tool to make things easy.

3) **Fine tune** your categories. Do you need to break down a category? Spending at places like Target, Walmart, or Amazon can be challenging (i.e., groceries and clothes on the same receipt). Maybe starting out, they are their own categories. Moving forward, it's worth looking at the breakdown and making adjustments that provide more information.

4) **Is your lifestyle reflected in your spending?** In other words, when you look at your money flow, does it support activities that bring you joy? Does it better your life?

5) Watch out for **impulse buys**. Before making the purchase, ask yourself, will this bring me joy? Does it support my lifestyle

and overall goal of financial independence? Would this spend better serve me in another area?

6) Don't forget to **record cash spending**. This is the only manual entry if you are using a budgeting app. Remember to record at the end of the day.

7) After 2-3 months, **analyze the flow** of money. At the end of each month total up all income, then subtract all spending. Was there money left over? Were there any surprises? Were there opportunities to lower spending? Most people are surprised at how much goes to restaurants, groceries, and discretionary categories (such as entertainment and travel).

8) **Challenge yourself** to cut excess spending in areas that don't bring you joy and funnel that money to areas that do.

9) **Treat Yourself.** That's right, remember to treat yourself. All successful diets have a little celebration.

3) Checking Your Credit Score

These days almost any financial institution, from banks to credit card companies, will give you your credit score for free. Credit scores, also known as FICO or Fair Isaac Corporation scores, are important because a higher score can translate into availability of and a better interest rate on loans.

If you have a Fair or Poor credit score, then lenders are not as likely to extend a loan. However, if a loan is extended, they will mitigate their risk by charging you a higher interest rate. That way, if you default, they will at least have had the opportunity to make some money on the loan.

According to Wallet Hub, credit score ranges are as follows:

• A score of 720 or higher is generally considered excellent credit.
• A score between 690 and 719 is considered good credit.

- Scores between 630 and 689 are fair credit.
- And scores of 629 or below are poor credit.

FICO Scores are calculated using many different pieces of credit data in your credit report. This data is grouped into five categories: payment history (35%), amounts owed (30%), length of credit history (15%), new credit (10%) and credit mix (10%).
myFICO

How do you improve your credit score? According to myFICO, the biggest bang for the buck is **to pay bills on time and in full.**

This is so important; it is first and second on the priority list and labeled as *payment history* making up 35% of a credit score. If you have a low score, start here.

The third most important thing to consider is your *amount owed, or total debt,* which is weighted at 30%. This should never be higher than 30% of total gross income. The lower the percentage, the better your credit score. Lowering the overall amount of debt will help in this area.

Your Turn

Take a moment and check your credit score through your bank or credit card company. If your credit score could use some improvement, this next exercise of pulling your credit history is the first step in building an excellent credit score. Remember, having the best credit score possible will put you in a strong position when opportunity knocks.

4) Examine Your Credit History

Credit history is a list of all financial debts and assets obtained over the last seven years. Annualcreditreport.com is a website that provides a free credit report every twelve months from the three main companies: *TransUnion, Experian,* and *Equifax.*

You can pull all three reports at the same time annually or one report every four months. If you are looking to build your credit score, then it may be helpful to pull one every four months to help guide you on where to focus your energy next. Keeping your credit report clean is another way to improve your credit score.

There is no better time than now to get rid of debt. Rip the Band-Aid off, raise your standards, and commit to getting organized.

Your Turn

Here are some simple steps to get you started.

1) Verify the information on your credit report is true and accurate.
2) Dispute anything that is inaccurate or not yours at all. Keep records of who you talk to, when, and about what. Keep copies of any written communications and replies.
3) Make a spreadsheet listing all debt with the following columns: Company, Payoff Amount, Interest Rate, Minimum Payment, Due On, and Accrued On.

Go to **grabyourslice.com/debt-buster-tracker-sample** to see an example.

Now that you know how much debt you have you can start to get rid of it. We'll tackle that in the next phase.

If you are proficient at Microsoft Excel and would like to get all the templates I have used (and still use) on my FI journey, go to **GrabYourSlice.com** and sign up to have them mailed to your Inbox.

PHASE TWO:
TOOLS AND DIRECTIONS

I have learned over the years that when one's
mind is made up, this diminishes fear; knowing
what must be done does away with fear.

Rosa Parks

Armed with my *why* (able to pay my bills and take a vacation or two without relying on a paycheck), S.M.A.R.T. goals, and FI crust (net worth, cash flow, credit score, and credit history), I was ready to start a new phase of my journey.

One of my goals was to sell the current house and downsize to lower the mortgage and monthly expenses. But before I could sell the house, I needed to purge the house. Going from big to small(er), I knew I couldn't take it all with me. Besides, cash was easier to pack and move than boxes of stuff I wouldn't have room for or need.

Cash was easier to pack and move than boxes
of stuff I wouldn't have room for or need.

Phase Two was about starting with the easy wins that would bring high returns with minimal effort. Having some quick wins not only gave me satisfaction but it also motivated me to keep moving forward.

YEAR TWO AND THREE: THE PURGE

With newfound confidence from surviving my first year on my own, I was ready to start pulling things together. If I had to pick a song to best describe the first part of this phase, it would be Stronger (What Doesn't Kill You) by Kelly Clarkson. I rolled up my sleeves and got started.

Clear the Clutter

Since I started Year Two unemployed, the first order of business was to prepare to downsize while continuing my job hunt. Maybe clearing out the house was a little premature. I didn't have a new house picked out and hadn't sold my current one. But I was unemployed and had time on my hands. I knew when I finally found a job, I would not be able to give this task the attention it needed. Purging the house was a project that, by myself, I knew was going to take many months and many passes.

The housing market was a buyers' market, which meant that as a seller, if I put my house for sale, I would get pennies on the dollar. I couldn't afford to "give" my house away. I needed every penny to pay off my debt and put a decent amount down on my next smaller home. Between that and the kids needing some stability, I decided to stay in the house another year. It was a gamble to see if the housing market would turn around. It was a gamble I was willing to take.

I focused on what I could control: purging the house. It was amazing how much stuff we accumulated. My plan of attack was to focus on one room at a time, focusing on the rooms we used the least. My starting point was the attic. It was almost full of boxes we forgot about. When the attic was all but empty, I turned my attention to the next room to clear out. I would go room-by-room with no mercy. The purge buckets were simple: Keep. Donate. Regift. Sell. Recycle. Trash. When I got to the garage, I added a bucket: Return. There was stuff in the garage that hadn't even been taken out of the box. Good grief!

What I learned was:

1) We had A LOT of stuff we didn't need or use.
2) The kids never noticed that the house was getting lighter.
3) There is no time like the present to get started.
4) Cash is easier to move to a new house than stuff.

During this time, it felt like there was little I could do to get out from under the crushing debt. Unemployment did not pay well and when I had a job, it was temporary work. The pay was only enough to cover expenses and a little extra (which I used to replenish my rainy-day fund). I felt it was more important to keep a solid rainy-day fund instead of paying down the debt, since the situation was uncertain. Knowing that we had that fund allowed me to sleep at night.

Mid-year, I found another contract job and again stayed committed to the decision of *paying myself first*. I added to my rainy-day fund and newly opened 401(k) with each paycheck. The debt would have to wait for now because I didn't know how long this job would last or if it would turn permanent. I also had no idea how long it would take to find another job if this one ended. Paying myself first was a requirement.

Without the kids, my financial decisions would have been different. I would have probably sold the house for whatever I could get and moved away with the clothes on my back. Being responsible for two more lives made me more accountable. I wanted so much for them, more than I wanted for myself and was willing to do whatever it took to get us out of the situation we were in.

Refinance

Having employment gave me an opportunity to refinance the home mortgage. The HELOC (Home Equity Line of Credit) debt was weighing me down and growing a little more each month since I was only paying the minimum required. I made the decision to refinance the home mortgage and roll in the HELOC balance, closing costs, and property taxes for the year into one mortgage and one monthly payment. Also, by doing this, it created the opportunity to put the loan and title in my name only. Having the house title in my name would pay off down the road when it came time to sell the house and handle all the paperwork in a timely fashion.

The new mortgage balance came out to about $259,000. My new monthly payment came to $1,326 per month, not including taxes and insurance. While refinancing didn't do anything for me in the short term, it made the most sense when I took the long view.

Budget 2.0

In Phase One, I spent a lot of time disciplining myself to record my cash flow without changing any habits. The first pass at budgeting was to set categories based on my cash flow and adjust as I learned new things about my spending. Building my budget tool was not a one-and-done activity. With every year, I learned new things and used that new information to refine my budgeting tool. Go to **GrabYourSlice.com** and sign up to receive freebie templates, like the MS Excel Budgeting tool I still use to this day.

My second pass was where the magic really started to happen. In budgeting 2.0, I did a deep dive in analyzing where I could or should cut spending and put that "extra" money towards a different category. I could also see the direct link between day-to-day cash flow and net worth. Budgeting became a critical tool in my FI toolbox.

Armed with some data from the last year, I made a first pass at creating budget 2.0 that reflected what I would spend. My biggest "a-ha" moment was seeing the impact of one-time expenses to my budget.

This year, when I created budget 2.0, I took one-time expenses into consideration more consistently and added more fun. If I wanted to take the kids to visit my mom, that was added to the budget and earmarked in the month it would be spent, while budgeting a little extra every month towards that one-time expense. These one-time expenses were never thought of before. Initially, part of my failure at budgeting was around the preconceived notion that all months were created equal, when in fact, they were not. As I learned more about budgeting, it became clear that it was a powerful tool when implemented correctly and not something to be feared.

The biggest thing I learned was how important it was to compare each month's spending and income and how it impacted the overall annual budget for that category. Looking at my monthly spending like this gave me new insights and flexibility. I found myself running my house like a small business, examining each expenditure against the goals for the year. *Did the spend put me a step closer to my overall goal or further back?* Looking at my finances in this light, gave me such confidence. This was empowering.

With the new mindset I made the following major changes:

- **Forecasted Monthly** and **Annual Budget** Columns: I kept the monthly budget (forecast) column and added an annual budget (forecast) column, basically multiplying the month amount times 12. This really drove things home on how much things would cost if I kept up with certain monthly spending.

- **Actual Monthly** and **Total Spend** Columns: I added a column for each month and an annual spend column that totaled up the <u>actual</u> spend in each monthly column. This would now show me how actual spending compared to budgeted or forecasted spending.
- **New/Updated Categories**: The last change I made was to group my spending. For example, all the house expenses were listed together, all the utility bills grouped, etc. I started my budget based on last year's spending with some adjustments for things I knew would come in the new year. It was not perfect but that was okay, I just needed a starting point and would adjust as I learned more.

With this information, I could:

- Have a bird's eye view of expenses projected for the new year, (i.e., how much my monthly spend would total by the end of the year).
- Clearly see the flow of money by category month-to-month.
- Reel in next month's spending in a category if I went over budget in the current month.
- Check in at the 6-month mark and make any forecasted adjustments based on actual spending.
- Clearly track emergency spending or windfalls (example, tax refund) and how it impacted the bottom line.

Lastly, because I took the time to really understand my cash flow, I didn't worry about overspending. If an emergency came up, the last thing I stressed about was having the money to cover the surprise expense.

Mid-Year Check-In

By mid-year, I had enough information to review my spending and income. In the early years, I was always looking for ways to improve my budgeting and goal setting skills. I asked myself questions like, was I on target for the year? Did I over/under spend? If so, why? Comparing my spending against what I budgeted gave me a ton of insight. Not only did I have a better understanding of where my money was going, but I would also trim the excess in areas that did not enhance my life and repurposed that money into areas that brought me joy. My biggest lesson here was how my everyday decisions impacted my bottom line.

I noticed little things, like how packing lunch contributed to my savings just as much as overspending took away from that same savings. From that moment on, I consciously chose to either spend on stuff or put that money towards building a retirement nest egg.

Forecasting

Another insight I gained was where big spends would be in the year. For example, March would have some extra spending to sign up for summer camp programs. Or maybe there would be a bump in groceries to make a birthday extra special.

Laying things out for the year gave me a bird's eye view of the flow of money I could expect. I could see very clearly the relationship between spending and happiness. Every month I would analyze the previous month and determine if I maximized my happiness. It became a game, a sort of "stealing from Peter to pay Paul". The best part was that I was in control.

I wasn't making more money but the money I did have coming in was maximized for optimal use. This is when I truly understood what was meant by *it doesn't matter how much you make, but what you do with what you have.*

*I understood that if I couldn't manage
small sums now, I was not going to be
ready to manage larger sums later.*

This, I learned, was the true way to budget. Before, when I would hear the word *budget*, the blood from my face would drain and a feeling of dread would overwhelm me. My thoughts would immediately be consumed with "going without fun," "having less," or "being restricted." Okay, yes, I am being a little over the top, but not by much. Handling money in this new-to-me way showed how wrong I was.

If I could keep my spending low, I would treat myself by squeezing in a trip or two. Using miles to buy airline tickets and couch surfing on friends' sofas made for quick cheap trips. Not to mention flying to mom's house and borrowing her car to get around town (and eat the food in her fridge – none of us ever get too old for that).

Emergency Expenses

Emergencies happen to all of us, and they never pop up on our calendar ahead of time. For example, our house had 2 HVAC units (upstairs and downstairs) which I had serviced at the end of Year Two. The upstairs unit was super old, and we knew when we bought the house that it would only be a matter of time before it needed to be replaced. My plan was to sell the house before this became an issue.

At the end of the year, I had the HVAC systems serviced. After looking at both systems, the repairman told me to replace the upstairs unit ASAP. The system was so old, he hadn't even seen this model in years! Not only that, but he was afraid if we turned it on, we could potentially be releasing carbon monoxide into the air. Yes, the repairman was saving our lives.

After the initial shock wore off, I was grateful I made the HVAC maintenance a priority. But how was I going to pay for a new HVAC unit? I wasn't quite sure yet. I couldn't take out a loan to make the repairs since I just refinanced the mortgage and consolidated my house debt. I had money in my rainy-day fund, but I wasn't prepared to spend this much out of it all at once.

Suddenly, I envisioned the three of us "camping" in the downstairs living room, with a fort and sleeping bags, like an adventure. Forgoing all electricity use to cut that bill as low as possible. Maybe that would buy me some time to scrape the money together, I thought. Then I came to my senses.

After some research on HVAC replacements, I found one model that offered a $1,500 tax credit and $300 rebate. Because we knew the HVAC would be an expensive replacement, as part of the divorce agreement, we would split the expense. The new HVAC unit with installation and hauling away old unit, came out to roughly $6,600.

New HVAC Replacement	$	6,600.00
50% from Divorce Agreement	$	(3,300.00)
Tax line Credit	$	(1,500.00)
Rebate	$	(300.00)
Subtotal	**$**	**1,500.00**

Then, one of those credit card offers came in the mail, offering a bunch of airline miles and 0% interest for the first few months. I decided to sign up for it and let my kids' dad know it was time to replace the upstairs HVAC. I sent him a copy of the bill for his records, and he gave me a check for $3,300.

The credit card came in and I charged the entire $6,600. Out of pocket, I spent $3,300 for a brand-new HVAC unit plus I got a couple of airline tickets, a check for $300 from the rebate, and a $1,500 tax credit at tax time out of it as a bonus. I was well on my way to becoming that financial magician just like my mom and…IT. FELT. GREAT.

About halfway through Year Three, my contract job ended. Focusing on what I could control, I picked up where I left off on my home purging project, filed for unemployment and started my job search. By the end of the summer, I was ready to put the house on the market.

I called and made an appointment to meet with the Realtor the following week. The house was cleaned up and my budget was updated. The Realtor arrived, I gave her a tour of the house, answered her questions, and then sat down to talk numbers.

We sat together, me with my laptop and budget, her with her notebook. She started by complimenting the house and all the upgrades completed but noted there was still work to be done. Then her tone turned serious.

In a nutshell, she explained that the housing market continued to be a challenge and backed that statement up with a noticeably short list of home comps in the area that sold within the last 18-months. Bottom line, I couldn't afford to sell the house, even with downsizing.

While it was not entirely surprising, it was still heartbreaking news. I mean, it's one thing to think it in your head, but quite another when someone in the business confirms your fear.

We moved on to Plan B: renting out the house and moving into a small rental to give the market a chance to turn around while lowering my monthly expenses. Going over those comps, she explained that the maximum rent I could collect would not cover the mortgage, taxes, and insurance, not to mention maintenance and upkeep. She calculated on a good month with no maintenance costs, I could potentially lose $100-$200 per month.

Lastly, she asked if I would be willing to rent out the guest room (Plan C). But I told her with two little kids in the house, I was uncomfortable with the idea of a stranger living with us.

The whole conversation was simultaneously heartbreaking and frustrating. I had a plan (and a backup plan). I had all my numbers. This time, I was ready, or at least I thought I was. The Realtor truly went above and beyond her role as real estate agent. I guess she could see that I needed all the support I could get.

I started to cry and apologized to the Realtor while pulling myself together. The Realtor explained there was nothing to apologize for and the situation was only temporary. She strongly felt the housing market would turn around, we just needed to be patient a little longer and keep an eye on things. She encouraged me to continue to purge and be ready to downsize when the opportunity presented itself.

Introduction to Rental Properties

Speaking of opportunity, the Realtor shared with me that she and her partner bought their first rental property in what they considered to be an up-and-coming part of town. We talked about the risks involved and how it was going. I had come across rental properties in my reading about passive income but didn't spend a lot of time on the topic, as it sounded complicated. Hearing her talk about their journey and dipping a toe in the rental property market gave me hope. With that, we said our goodbyes and planned to touch base every few months and check to see if it was a better time to put the house on the market.

As agreed, every few months, we checked in with each other to take a temperature on the housing market. We would also talk about how their first rental property purchase was going. In a nutshell, it was awful. Every mistake that could be made was made in that first rental. But it proved to be fertile ground to learn the business from the ground up which paid off in spades. With their purchase of each new rental property, they refined the process and eventually turned this knowledge into a side business finding rentals for investors looking to build their own rental property portfolio.

Watching and listening to their story made me feel like I could maybe do this too. So, I started to add books to read on real estate and rental properties to my nightstand starting with the *Rich Dad, Poor Dad* series. This was another opportunity to learn about rental property as an income stream for myself.

Books about how to build different streams of passive income became my nightly ritual reading. The more I learned about passive income the more excited I was at the possibility of making my own FI Pie filling. The education I was building went towards preparing myself for when opportunity knocked and eventually, I knew it would.

Changing my Money Mindset

I want to take a moment and pause here because it may seem like not much has happened for the first three years of this journey. The struggle and stress to find work and periodically living on unemployment was taking its toll mentally, emotionally, and physically. Each year when I calculated my net worth it was slightly less than the previous year.

At one point my son came to me and asked, "Mommy, are we poor?" I sat him down and explained that we were not because we had a roof over our heads, clothes on our backs, and food on the table. So long as we had that and each other, we were good.

The truth was, I was worried. I am not going to lie, there were nights, after the kids would go to bed, I would go to my room and cry. Living paycheck-to-paycheck on the best of months was stressful enough. Living on unemployment was demoralizing. It felt like life moved on without me. What happened to my plan of living happily ever after with a budding career of one promotion (and salary increase) after another?

Life can be unfair. That is the plain hard truth. We all have stories of struggle and triumph. Being in the middle of difficult times, it was hard to have faith that success was just around the corner. During the down times, I would lean hard on my *why* and commitment to being financially independent. It was at the forefront of my mind and guided every decision I made. Through perseverance and grit, I kept my commitment to do better for me and the kids.

These three years were spent leveraging what I did have within my control: time and courage. Time to learn the tools to leverage the money I did have. Time to educate myself on the different paths to financial independence. Time to put myself in the strongest position possible so when opportunity knocked on my door, I would be ready to open it. And the courage to make it all come together.

Every day was a baby step towards building that solid crust on which the perfect FI Pie filling would be supported. Every day was a decision of priorities. Pack lunch or buy? Pay retail or wait for a sale? Pay debt or fund rainy-day account? Watch free movie at home or buy movie theater tickets?

I finally understood that money is really nothing more than a tool. A powerful tool that, if used correctly, would get me to where I needed to be. And I needed to be free. Free from debt. Free to live my authentic life.

During the first few months, it didn't seem like any of these mini choices made a difference. Over time, what I was building were my FI tools. No one could take those away from me. That was empowering. I was clearing my FI pantry to make room for the right FI ingredients and tools. In the moment, it was hard to understand that. But when opportunity finally did come, I was ready.

> *If you don't want to be average, don't rush*
> *into doing what the crown is doing.*
> **Constance Chuks Friday**

Lessons Learned

- Anything worth doing is worth doing right. The numbers were not anything to brag about, but they did start to tell a story. There is power in knowledge.
- Delayed gratification can be powerful. I could have sold the house and taken a major loss in the name of moving forward. Taking the emotion out of the equation gave me clarity.
- Don't waste time and money keeping up with the Joneses (instead borrow their pool, it's cheaper).

Year End Summary

During these two years I focused on what I could control, which was to get myself to as strong a position as possible so I would be ready when opportunity came. My net worth dropped about $5,000 from Year One, which wasn't a surprise given my on-again, off-again relationship with unemployment and ultra conservative investing practices. But I consolidated my debt, which put me in a stronger position to make autonomous decisions when opportunity came along. In other words, what became very clear was that if I was going to find my perfect FI Pie recipe, I needed to make sure I was not dependent on anyone else giving me the ingredients. To see details, go to **grabyourslice.com/year-two-and-three.**

YEAR FOUR: DOWNSIZE AND STREAMLINE LIFE

Year Four was a bit of a roller coaster but also the year everything started to change for the better. I could breathe again. Not only that, but all that preparing for opportunity was well worth it. This year was a cross between Mary Chapin Carpenter's The Bug and Diana Ross' I'm Coming Out.

It was another year and another contract job. I continued the theme of "pay myself first" and signed up for the 401(k) even though there was no match. At the end of each contract job, I would take that 401(k) invested money and roll it into my IRA. This was always important to do because 1) it would be easy to forget that 401(k) money was there, and 2) by rolling over, instead of cashing out, I avoided paying taxes and steep penalties. By consolidating under an IRA, it made it much easier to manage and invest.

I also continued to purge my house and monitor the housing market for any signs that it was time to sell. The beginning of the year was quiet as it normally is coming off the holidays. To be honest, I didn't really care what my house sold for. If I got enough out of it to buy a smaller house, pay off my debts, and lower my overall cost of living, I was all in.

Opportunity Knocked

Then, that spring, it finally happened. The housing market was showing signs of a possible turnaround. I called my Realtor and together we decided now was the time to list the house.

I knew this was not going to be the same experience I had the first time when we sold our house in California. There would be no multiple offers, each one outbidding the other. I wouldn't be coming away with that feeling of winning the lottery. This time the housing market was fragile, with very few buyers and a ton of homes for sale.

Nonetheless, I was ready. I had purged the house to remove clutter and pocketed the cash. I educated myself on real estate and spent time planning the next steps after I downsized. Plus, I had a great Realtor on my side. It wasn't easy. Buyers knew the market was in their favor and some took advantage of that. Some only gave 30-minutes notice for a showing, which gave me barely enough time to prep the house, grab the kids, and get out for an hour to give them time to walk through.

In the meantime, we went looking for my new downsized home. It took exactly two weekends, when we came across a small new development, with only about 40 homes and six different floor plans. There was one home left in the neighborhood that fit my criteria and price point, a 3-bedroom, 2.5-bath with about 2,000 square feet, listed at $235,000 ($117.50 per square foot).

I remember it as if it were yesterday. We went and saw it on a Saturday. I loved the home and its layout, and the neighborhood was perfect for raising kids. The location could not have been better with elementary, middle, and high schools all within a 5- to 10-minute drive. After a short talk with my Realtor, I decided to put in an offer for the asking price, which she would submit Monday morning. *Slam dunk*, I thought. The house was as good as officially mine.

Monday afternoon, my Realtor called to give me an update. My offer was rejected.

Now, you must be wondering, how can they reject it, you offered the asking price? True, you read it correctly, we did offer the asking price. Apparently, the builder hired a new Head of Sales that started the week before. His first order of business was to increase the price on that model and allegedly, got it approved on that Sunday. The new price was now $10,000 more.

Purchase Price of Downsize	$	235,000.00
30yr Fixed Loan @ 3.75%	$	120,000.00
Down Payment	$	115,000.00

I was heartbroken. My Realtor was outraged. I told her to let it go, that maybe it wasn't meant to be. The truth was, I didn't have it in me for a battle. But she wouldn't hear of it. She saw the look on my face when we walked through and knew this was the house and neighborhood for me and my kids. The battle between my Realtor and the builder went on for weeks. My Realtor was amazing. She took her argument up the builder's management chain and stopped short of reaching out to the CEO. They finally accepted our original offer noting they were "throwing in" $10,000 worth of upgrades. Now we just needed to sell my house so I could move.

I was in overdrive, working to continue to sell off as much stuff as possible. Less to pack and more cash to pocket. Thank goodness I started this process early on. Even though plenty was gone, there was still a lot to go through.

Life Happens

Then, as Murphy's Law would have it, my car died. I had it towed to my long-time mechanic and sat in the waiting room like an expectant parent, wondering if "my baby" was going to be alright.

Finally, the mechanic came out. He said "this car is a money pit. You need to get rid of it. Find yourself a used Honda with less than

100,000 miles on it. Trade this one in, they will sell it for parts and make a profit as this model is discontinued."

"Are you kidding me?" I thought. "I am in the middle of moving with two little kids and now I need to go car shopping?"

I did not have the money to buy a car, used or otherwise. I had no idea what I was going to do. I went to my tax accountant for advice. I explained the situation, and how repairing the car was not an option.

After listening patiently, his reply was matter of fact. "You can't afford to take out a loan", he said. "You have no collateral. Find a cheap car and under no circumstances take out a loan."

"Are you kidding me?" I thought. "I am trying my best to get my finances back on track and now I need to figure out how to squeeze in a car purchase with no car loan?"

I didn't have the time to haggle, so I went to CarMax, armed with my car criteria. A salesman met me at the door with a smile and asked what brought me in today. I told him I was looking for a Honda with 4 doors and less than 100,000 miles on it.

He asked what color I had in mind. I wondered whether men get asked this question? But I just told him it didn't really matter.

He smiled and said, "I am sure we have what you are looking for." Then turned and started walking towards the sea of used cars.

"Hold on there," I said. "I just gave you my criteria, can't we just go inside and look it up?"

As he turned to look at me, he nodded in agreement and with that we went inside. He led me to a small conference room and asked me to take a seat. He sat at the desk facing me, punching in my criteria on the computer. Just like that one car popped up. Only one. A Honda Civic 4-door with less than 100,000 miles. It was just an hour away and became available only two days earlier. The cost was about $12,350. That was a lot of money when I couldn't take out a loan. It was time to leverage my financial magician abilities and somehow buy this car with no loan.

As it turned out, they valued my trade-in at $5,000. Great!

$7,350 to go.

After selling a ton of stuff on Craigslist and at garage sales, I had about $5,000 in cash.

Down to $2,350.

Because I was paying in full, they gave me a $50.00 discount. (Hey, it's better than a stick in the eye.)

Down to $2,300.

I pulled out my checkbook and wrote a check for the remaining amount, pulling the money from my rainy-day fund.

The kids gave a teary goodbye to our old car and lukewarm hello to the Civic. Granted, the Civic was not sexy but it had great gas mileage and with 4 doors, a lot easier for the kids to get into and out of.

With the car situation settled and behind us, I was ready to refocus on selling the house.

Life Happens ... Again

We found a buyer for my house, negotiated the sale price, agreed on a date... and we moved early that summer with the help of friends. Easy as pie. Not exactly. I wish that happened!

There was a lot of back and forth with the buyers. They knew they had the upper hand in the challenging real estate market. Negotiations were brutal, they squeezed me for every dime they could, until we finally agreed on a price of $395,000, roughly $130.15 per square foot. It was a 60-day closing, longer than the traditional 30-days. I didn't have much of a choice and agreed on the terms of the sale.

List Price of the Big House	$	425,000.00
Sale Price	$	395,000.00
5% commission and closing co	$	(19,750.00)
Misc Repairs	$	(8,000.00)
Mortgage Balance	$	(252,000.00)
Cash Balance	**$**	**115,250.00**

Fast forward to closing day and we packed what was left on one moving truck with the help of friends. I was ready that afternoon to drive the truck to my new home and begin unpacking. Then I got a call from my Realtor. The closing would be delayed. That's right, after the buyer asked for a 60-day closing they were still not ready.

Completely irritated, my Realtor explained that the buyers were missing one piece of paper, required for official transfer of property. It turns out, not only were they missing it, but they needed another week to get it. Another week!

Then my Realtor let me know that not only did they need another week, but they had the nerve to expect me to move out, as planned, and hand over the keys. When I asked about the closing and exchange of funds, my Realtor asked the same question. The buyer's Realtor said they *promised* to complete the closing one week after the original closing date.

These were the same people who did everything they could to make this process as painful as possible. There was no way I was going to trust them just because they said they would have all their paperwork in order and transfer funds a week after they moved in. My Realtor and I agreed we would not hand over the keys until all paperwork was completed, and monies transferred.

The truck and all our worldly possessions would sit at the foot of the driveway until all the paperwork was in order, signed, and the check cleared. And it did, in fact, take a full week. Since the house was completely packed and I couldn't move the truck, I had nowhere to live. Without the transfer of money from the closing, I couldn't close and get the keys to my new home. In effect, I was in limbo. Lucky that I planned to close and move the week the kids would be at their dad's. I ended up staying at a friend's house. The buyers paid the extra week for the truck rental.

Creating Opportunity

Once I moved, I opened a new Home Equity Line of Credit (HELOC) against the equity in my new house. Now, I know what you're thinking. *Monica, you just spent four years trying to get out of debt and yet you went and got another loan?!* But I had a very good reason and a plan to use this HELOC as leverage. There would be no blind spending this time around.

The bank approved my HELOC for $82,000. My plan was to leverage the equity in my new home to buy rental properties. It was risky but this time it was a calculated risk I was willing to take. This was the opportunity I was waiting for to add to my small but growing FI Pie filling.

That weekend the kids settled into their new rooms. Eventually, the rest of the house came together, unpacking the last of the boxes. That first day, waking up in my new home with my debt substantially decreased by about half, I felt as though I could breathe again. It felt amazing. The sale of the old house at $395,000 was enough to not only pay the old mortgage in full, but it also gave me enough to put half down on the new house and have a new mortgage of $120,000.

I spent the second half of year planning my next steps and reading more financial and real estate books. I wanted to be as prepared as possible to make my FI Pie filling and started a checklist of what I needed to do to build a real estate passive income stream.

Rental Property as a FI Pie Filling?

Through many conversations with my Realtor about their own journey of building a rental property portfolio and my own reading and research, I decided that to make rental properties a true passive income stream I would need to own at least three "doors" (properties, in real estate investor speak) to make it worth my time. But to make it profitable I would need to purchase at least five to as many as ten. This was based on what homes were selling and renting for and what I needed to cover in terms of monthly rental property expenses.

Leveraging my budgeting experience, I ran budget simulations to determine what would be a good fit for me based on what I could afford. I took into consideration known costs like, mortgage, taxes, insurance, and property management fees but went beyond that to factor in repairs, which were difficult to estimate. Even with all my own reading and research, you don't know what you are getting into sometimes.

I also asked myself a series of what-if questions like, what if I didn't have a renter for six months? What if I lost my job? With each question I adjusted the budget identifying potential risks and determined the best way to mitigate each one. With each question and budget refinement, I gleamed a little for knowledge of what I could do and where I needed to focus my attention.

I decided to beef up my rainy-day funds and worked closely with my Realtor and her property manager to understand all the risks with rental properties.

I also set up appointments with my banker, tax accountant, and insurance agent to gather more information and kept my Realtor and her property manager updated.

With each conversation, I explained my goal of purchasing between 5-10 rental properties, two a year starting the following year. I asked each of them what they needed from me to make this a reality.

My banker must have thought I was nuts. A single mom with no job (contract work does not count I learned), little available cash, and a HELOC with $82,000 credit limit. Honestly, you should have seen the look on his face. It was a cross between, "are you crazy?" and "why are you wasting my time?" But in the end, he played along and said to come back next year when I had my newly filed tax returns in hand. I didn't let his lack of enthusiasm deter me from making my best effort on this venture. I just took it as an action item and moved on.

My tax accountant has always been my friend and sounding board. I ran every small business idea I ever had by him. In truth, up until the real estate idea, he had shot them all down with plenty of facts to back him up. This was the first idea he supported, although maybe not the purchasing-two-every-year part.

He reminded me that real estate is not without its pitfalls and risks, and I could just as easily lose money. He advised me to start a Limited Liability Corporation (LLC) for extra protection and gave me the name of a long-time friend and lawyer who drew up the paperwork and at a reasonable price.

Lastly, my insurance agent just needed to know the name of the LLC and contact information for the property manager, then wished me luck. Really, he was happy for me but had no opinion on whether this was a sound investment or not.

I was on my way to building my first portfolio … of anything.

Portfolio. "How strange," I thought, "I am at a financial place in life where I can consider building a portfolio … of anything, let alone real estate."

I went over the plan in my head countless times, thinking about all the potential roadblocks there could be ahead and how I was going to handle each one. I was finally in the driver's seat with an opportunity of my own making. I thought about the conversations with my tax accountant, Realtor, and banker and the risk of real estate investing.

I reflected on how far I had come in just the first four years. This year was when all the debt from the marriage was paid in full. Not only that, but my new smaller home was already 50% paid for. I even had money in retirement accounts, an index fund, and a funded rainy-day savings account. Thinking about all that, I had to ask myself, was the reward of investing in rental properties worth the risk of losing it all? I had my kids to think about. If I moved forward, there was not much room for error.

I took a step back and made sure I understood the risk and reward. After weighing out the pros and cons for the umpteenth time, I decided I was all in and committed to my real estate plan. In the end, I thought that even though downsizing and being debt free was an incredible feeling, it wasn't enough to get me to MY definition of financial independence. I needed more than being debt free, I needed to build security in my life. I wanted the security in knowing that I would never again find myself in such a vulnerable position. After all that soul searching and number crunching, I set a new stretch goal for myself of purchasing two rental properties per year for a total of ten properties. It was a lot, to be sure, but if there was one thing I learned about myself, it's that I am very goal oriented. You don't know until you try.

Forgetting Balance

The last few years of stress started to catch up to me. One autumn day, I was on my way home from work and found myself almost nodding off while driving on the freeway. I opened the car windows and turned up the music to fight the urge to close my eyes. Initially, I shrugged it off, thinking I was only tired and needed a good night's sleep.

Night after night, I started sleeping 10-11 hours only to be tired the next day and wishing I could take a nap. It didn't take long to figure out I needed to take a break and made an appointment with my doctor. I let my manager know I needed a few days off and explained the situation. He said to take the time and to not worry about my temp job, it would be here when I was ready to come back. I rested and went to see my doctor. She did some blood tests and eventually diagnosed me with an autoimmune disease called Hashimoto's. It would take a few months to get the right medication dosage but once we did, and with the help of some lifestyle changes, I would be just fine.

After a few days off, I called my manager to say I was ready to come back to work. On the phone they told me that my contract had been terminated.

I was angry and scared. How long would it take to find another job that fit my single parent criteria, temp or otherwise? I felt betrayed. My mom flew out to help with the kids, cooking, and cleaning while I continued to recover.

Just as the year had started, I ended the year on unemployment. It was different this time. I had cut my monthly expenses and had a solid foundation to build on. These positive steps gave me confidence that we would be okay. It is because of this incident and the number of times I have been on unemployment that, to this day, I carry a larger-than-necessary rainy-day fund.

At this point, it may seem like not a lot had changed in my financial picture. I traded stuff for cash, down sized, and changed out my car. But in truth, I lowered my overall debt by $121,000. I lowered my monthly expenses by a few hundred dollars just on the mortgage and utilities.

More importantly, what I learned in these few short years was invaluable. It laid a solid foundation for all the opportunities and events that would come.

I needed to be patient and continued to focus on what I could do daily to take a step towards financial independence. This gave me control over my life and that, in and of itself, was life changing.

Rome wasn't built in a day. Mountains are not climbed in a moment.

I used all these tools at different points during these years and I used them in different ways. What it gave me was the start of a picture of what I had to work with, where my deficiencies were, and what options I had in front of me. It gave me the power and confidence to make my own destiny.

I always want to stay focused on who I am,
even as I'm discovering who I am.
Alicia Keys

Lessons Learned

- Downsize and Streamline. One of the best ways I found to make some extra money was to sell as much stuff as possible and generally streamline my life to be responsible for less.
- Track Cash Flow. Tracking cash flow was one of the most empowering things I did for myself as it helped me to handle problems as they occurred with minimal financial impact to our day-to-day living.
- Be aware and flexible. Reviewing my goals and keeping my intentions clear kept me on course. I was able to update and pivot as I learned more, which allowed me to get the most out of each year.

Year End Summary

Even though my overall net worth went down a little more, I considered Year Four a big step forward in my overarching plan to achieve financial independence. For one thing, I downsized and lowered my month-to-month expenses not to mention my responsibilities. Second, I was able to get a new-to-me car without a car loan—an empowering move to say the least. Third, I purchased my first home on my own. Fourth, I opened a credit card with zero interest to purchase things for the house, thereby leveraging credit with purpose, with a plan to pay off the balance in full before the interest-free period was over. It was a rollercoaster year but with more ups than downs. To see details, go to **grabyourslice.com/year-four**.

Directions

Every pie recipe has a specific list of ingredients and corresponding directions. You can't just throw everything in a bowl without thinking of the order that would yield the best crust and filling. Baking is more science than art, which is why it's important to take a moment and make sure you have all the right ingredients ready and available.

Making a FI Pie is very similar. We have the basic crust ingredients laid out from Phase One. What I have learned from my own journey was that making the basic crust was a great starting point. But the magic really happened when I took the crust recipe and modified it to support my perfect-for-me FI Pie filling. In this phase, I have a list of directions that can take your basic FI Pie crust to the next level.

How to Boost Net Worth - Instantly

If you are looking for ways to give your net worth a raise here are some things to try:

- **Spring Cleaning.** Get rid of the clutter. Not only will your home feel lighter but there will be less to clean and maintain. Sell stuff you don't use or doesn't support the lifestyle you want. You would be amazed at how much cash you can make. Don't underestimate this. The more stuff you have the more it costs to maintain and the more space you need to store it, which brings me to my next point.

- **Downsize.** Do you really need all this space? Maybe the "Joneses" do, but that doesn't mean you need it as well. Remember the more roof over your head, the more it costs month over month to maintain. Even if you are renting a place, downsizing can be a money saver. Think about it like this, $1,500/month in rent is $18,000 per year. It adds up quickly. It's worth looking into.

- **Refinance.** At the time of this writing, mortgage rates in the US were low. Look at refinancing from a 30 year to a 20 or even 15-year loan. You may have a slightly higher monthly payment but the savings in interest and years off the loan may be worth it. It costs nothing to explore all options before deciding.
- **Unclaimed Money.** In the United States, millions of dollars go unclaimed every year in the form of tax refunds, pension plans, life insurance, savings bonds, retirement benefits, utility deposits/refunds, and more. It may be worth the time to do a search. If you are in the United States, remember to expand your search to past states lived in. You may be surprised by what you find.

If you have already checked off some of the steps above, congratulations! Great job! How does it feel? Empowering, right?

Taking control of your finances impacts all areas of life, including health and mental well-being. As you move through the process, you'll start to feel a little lighter, stand a little taller, and feel a little more confident. Maybe you are already experiencing some of these shifts. If so, that is awesome! It only gets better from here. Keep building those financial muscles.

How to Get Rid of Debt

Debt can be debilitating and can keep you from moving forward. Below are five strategies to tackle debt. Read each one and determine which would work best for you.

1) **Avalanche**: Best for delayed gratification types. Focus on paying off the **highest** interest rate debt first, while still paying the minimum due for the rest of your balances. Once that debt is paid off, roll that amount to the next highest interest rate, until all debt is paid in full.

2) **Snowball**: Best for instant gratification types. Focus on paying off the **lowest** amount first, while still paying the minimum due for the rest of the loans. Once that first account is paid off, roll that amount to the next lowest amount, until all debt is paid in full.

3) **Consolidate**: Best for strategic and proactive types. Leverage a 0% credit card transfer for 12-18 months offers. Whatever the total amount transferred to the 0% card should be divided up by the number of months the 0% is good for. For example, if you have $2,000 in debt you are rolling onto a card that has a 0% interest rate for 12 months, you'll need to plan to pay $166.67 each month for the next 12 months so you can pay it off before fees hit.

4) **Debt Companies**: Best for those that do not want to handle negotiating with the credit card company for a smaller interest rate or balance. Everything is negotiable.

5) **Bankruptcy**: Really this should be avoided and only used as a last resort. Filing for bankruptcy wipes out all debt except medical and student loans. Also, you won't be allowed to purchase a home with a mortgage for the next seven years, not to mention the legal fees incurred. This is not to be taken lightly and only used as a very last resort.

If you have chosen one of the strategies above, you are ready to put your plan into action. Go through the following steps:

1) Pull out your list of debt from Phase One and reorganize it according to the strategy picked above.

2) Stay committed. Remember your *why* at the beginning of this journey.

3) Revisit your debt repayment plan often: daily, weekly, or monthly.

4) Challenge yourself. For example, brown bag lunch for a week and put that money towards debt repayment. Believe me when I say that every little bit adds up both in a positive and negative way.

5) Extra Motivation. Recalculate Net Worth after each debt is paid in full. Watch your debt shrink and net worth increase. This can be a big motivator. Revel in the amount of money saved just by not paying interest and late fees.

6) Extra incentive. Define small ways to celebrate each milestone hit. Make a list of little celebrations to look forward to. For example, maybe after brown bagging lunch for a week, you treat yourself to an inexpensive lunch out.

How to earn 16% (or more) instantly. The average interest rate on credit cards in the U.S. can be anywhere from 16% up to as high as 24% or more depending on how good (or bad) your FICO score is, according to Forbes Magazine. The fastest and easiest way to earn more than 16% interest is to **pay off your credit card debt**. Once you stop spending that amount on interest every month, you'll have that amount to start saving and investing. Charging *outrageous* interest rates (and late fees) is how credit card companies make their money. You are no longer their sugar mama (or papa). For example, those pairs of shoes that originally cost $100, paid for with a credit card, paid off over a series of months could end up being closer to a $200 pair of shoes. That is no exaggeration.

Getting rid of debt is a big step towards
lowering your overall spending and increasing
your overall savings and investing.

How to Pay Yourself First

The idea of paying yourself first sounds simple on the surface. But how do you get started? Do you pay yourself after all the necessary bills (rent and utilities)? Do you pay yourself the same amount every month? Where do you invest that money?

Paying yourself first, means paying yourself before even one bill gets paid for the month. Before rent/mortgage, utilities, car payments, etc. Paying yourself is the very first thing that gets done, without exception, and it happens consistently.

Pretax examples of paying yourself first are 401(k)s and Health Savings Accounts (HSAs). This is where the money from your paycheck goes into these accounts pre-tax. Leveraging these types of accounts lowers your overall tax bill since it does come out before taxes are paid.

Post-tax examples of paying yourself first are a savings or money market accounts, Index Fund/Mutual Fund, or a Roth IRA. When setting up an automatic deposit of your paycheck, you can split the net amount to multiple accounts. This is the safest way to ensure you pay yourself first.

Remember to fund a rainy-day account in the form of a savings or money market account. Once this is funded, divert the pay-yourself-first money to investments, like the examples above. You can calculate how much you need in your rainy-day fund based on 1) how secure your job is, 2) what big expenses are coming up, 3) what other income streams you can rely on, and 4) how much risk you feel comfortable taking.

Why am I making such a point of this? Because it's a critical concept to understand and adopt into your plan for financial independence and it ties directly with managing your flow of money. This concept helped me to turn around my financial life and I know it can help you too.

To implement paying yourself first successfully:

1) Start small and use percentages instead of a dollar amount.
2) Use direct deposit and automate payments by paycheck.
3) As you get comfortable, review your monthly spending and determine if you can increase your percentage.

If it's so easy, then why doesn't everyone pay themselves first? Do any of these sound like you?

- **Fear**. Fear of not having enough.
- **Trust**. Trust yourself enough to move forward and be okay when you make a mistake.
- **Instant Gratification**. Uncontrollable urge to shop without thought to how it will impact your finances.
- **No Plan**. Just throw your hands up and hope that everything will work out.
- **Spender**. Earn a dollar but spend two.
- **It's just not done**. Maybe your parents never trusted anyone with their money, and you grew up with the same thoughts. You work and stick any extra money in an envelope under the mattress.

Understanding *why* we do things is important. That insight helps in understanding how to move forward and get to the level we want and deserve.

Another way of paying yourself is by claiming free money when offered to you.

How to Collect Free Money

Let's say your boss calls you into her office. She pulls out a $50 bill and says, "To claim this $50, all you have to do is put $100 on the table and it's yours. You get to keep your $100 and the $50." What would you do? Pony up the $100!! It's a 50% return on investment (ROI). Well, many companies already do this in the form of an employer match contribution to your 401(k) plan.

If you are working for a company, take some time to review all the benefits offered. You would be surprised at the number of ways to claim free money that many people never take advantage of.

Review your company benefits package or check with the Benefits department to find out more ways your company offers free money.

Here are some of the most common cash investments and profitable ways of paying yourself first:

1) 401(k)

Most companies offer some type of match of your 401(k) investment. For example, the match could be $.50 for every dollar you invest up to 6% of your paycheck. That would be a 50% return right off the bat. Also, because this is pre-tax income (money spent before being taxed), know that in retirement, withdrawals will be taxed as ordinary income.

At a minimum, collect the company match. Never leave free money on the table. If you can, max out contributions to your 401(k) to what is allowed. Doing this would lower your overall tax bill. For 2022, the maximum allowed contribution for those under 50 years young is $20,500. Those 50 and older, have the option of contributing an additional, catch-up amount of $6,500 per year.

Keep in mind, you may have to stay at your company for a set number of years to retain their matched dollars. This is known as vesting. Once you are fully vested you keep all the money the company put into the account.

While my temp jobs had a 401(k), none of them offered a match. But I still invested because 1) it was good practice to pay myself first and 2) it lowered my overall taxable income.

2) Roth IRA

Roth IRA is also an excellent way to pay yourself first. Here you use post-tax money and let it grow tax free until retirement age. That means in retirement any withdrawals from the Roth are tax free. The longer the time horizon, the more the investment grows and the more you have in retirement. In 2022 the maximum contribution allowed is $6,000 with a catch-up contribution for those 50 and over of $1,000. Also, as of 2022, a single person would need to make less than $144,000 and a married couples combined incomes would need to be less than $208,000 to be eligible for the full contribution.

3) Health Savings Account (HSA)

The *Health Savings Account* or HSA is a favorite of mine. It's basically a checking account that only pays for medical expenses (see the IRS site for a full list of items covered). There are opportunities to invest this money in lower risk mutual funds. Like the 401(k), it uses pre-tax dollars, so there is more investing power, and most companies pay extra into your account. The best part: investments grow tax free. It's like a tax loophole for the average Joe or Jill.

HSAs are also known as a *triple tax threat* because again 1) no tax is paid on the money put into the account, 2) no tax is paid on any interest made, and 3) no tax is paid when the money is spent. There is literally nothing else like it.

So, what is the catch? There must be one, right? There are two small ones. First, you are again capped (all the good ones are) at how much is deposited each year. In 2022, the maximum contribution was $3,650. Second, to be eligible you must enroll in a high deductible health plan. This may not be for everyone. It's important to weigh the pros and cons for your specific situation.

When I was first eligible to sign up for an HSA, I did not take the time to fully understand or appreciate how amazing it is. As a result, I did not sign up for one right away. This is a small regret on my part. But when I finally did, in Year Nine of this journey, I maxed it out every year, and paid out of pocket for any medical expenses I had. This allowed the HSA to grow (since it rolls over year over year), and I could leverage it later when I am older and not collecting a paycheck.

Tools

Just like with your pie recipe, you'll likely take out all the tools you need *before* you start any mixing. You'll get out your bowls and measuring cups, your mixer and whisk, and make sure you have everything you need to get started.

Now that we have our crust ingredients and directions on the different ways to enhance it, here are the tools you'll need on the counter to not only make your crust, but to make your filling too.

Money

Yes, at the top of the list of tools is money. That is all money is: a tool used to build net worth and achieve your definition of financial independence.

Budget

Whether you use paper and pen, excel or a budgeting app, tracking your money flow and measuring that flow against the house budget is one of the most critical tools. It's the boots on the ground that dictates direction. Master budgeting and your net worth will grow.

Standards

You are on our way to building financial independence. To do that you need to raise your standards. Getting by, paycheck to paycheck, and carrying debt is no longer acceptable. You deserve better. Raise your standards and start looking at ways to add value to your life. Do your homework and look at different ways to create passive income streams that leverage your own skills and interests.

Commitment

Now that you have determined your starting point and pulled out the ingredients to make that perfect FI Pie crust, you are in a strong position to start building your pie filling. It's important to make that commitment to yourself and your family. Don't be discouraged by where you are right now. It's just a point in time. You have the power to make positive changes.

Grit and Perseverance

Grit (the courage to be better) plus perseverance (the ability to keep driving forward regardless of circumstances) equals a stronger, better you with the lifestyle you deserve. Without that get-up-and-go attitude and not letting anything stand in your way, the journey ends now. On those hard days, your *why* really comes in handy. Raise your life standards and commit to being better by using grit and perseverance each and every day to the best of your ability. You deserve nothing less.

Dollar Cost Averaging

Investopedia defines Dollar Cost Averaging as,

"An investment strategy in which an investor divides up the total amount to be invested across periodic purchases of a target asset in an effort to reduce the impact of volatility on the overall purchase. The purchases occur regardless of the asset's price and at regular intervals."

With dollar cost averaging, you put the money into the market on a set date no matter what. Whether the market is down or up you invest. You take the emotion and fear out of the equation. You invest money in the market and don't sweat it if there was a dip or not.

The most common example of dollar cost averaging is the 401(k). In a perfect world, I would have maxed this out every working year. The reality was, I invested what I could but sometimes I would forget to select the investment fund.

Mistakes I made:

1) Not automating paying yourself first with direct deposit.
2) Not leveraging the 401(k) to lower overall taxes.
3) Not collecting the company match (i.e., leaving money on the table).
4) Not investing in a fund (i.e., signing up for 401(k) and having it go to a savings or money market account).
5) Not investing for the long term.

My journey showed me that dollar cost averaging works, when investing for the long haul. The key is to put the money to work and not let it sit in a checking or savings account (not counting the rainy-day funds).

Tools: But Wait There's More...

Throughout the years of my self-imposed financial education from various books, blogs, and online articles, I came across several rules and guidelines that helped me along the way and shaped how I manage my finances. Below is a sample:

1) **50-30-20 Rule**. My dad mentioned this to me early on. This basic rule of thumb states to use 50% of your income on basic living expenses (needs), 30% for fun (wants), 20% for savings. Over the years a few variations evolved:

   - 50-30-10-10 to include 10% for tithing.
   - 30-20-50 The FIRE version flips this rule around and uses 30% on needs, 20% wants, and 50% on savings.

   In the end, it doesn't really matter which way your monthly income is sliced up. What is important is that a percentage of it goes towards savings and investing every month, just like paying rent or a mortgage. The earlier you start the better the returns.

2) **Three Ways to Save More Money**. This is one I was excited about since it gave me options to get control over my money and time.

   a) *Lower Expenses*. This was the easiest way I was able to pick up extra cash. By just monitoring my spending and seeing where I could spend less, I automatically freed up money to invest. Also, just by downsizing, I was able to save hundreds in monthly spending on utilities and mortgage.

b) *Earn More.* I did a little bit of this by picking up various side gigs. I would house sit, make meals, teach pasta making, and babysit.

c) *Work Longer.* For me, this was in the form of working overtime when I worked contract jobs. But it can also include working in retirement years instead of taking traditional retirement.

3) **Debt Limit**. My personal rule of thumb is to keep total debt (mortgage and other) at 20% of total combined credit limits but preferably as low as possible. Most mortgage companies will advise total debt to be no higher than 36% of total combined credit limits.

4) **Student Loan Debt**. Rule of thumb is the total loan should max out at less than or equal to your first year's salary in that profession.

5) **Debt-to-income Ratio**. This compares the amount of money that goes toward debt repayment and monthly take-home pay by dividing the monthly debt by monthly income. The lower the number the better. As a rule of thumb, anything higher than a 36% may cause higher interest rate loans.

For me, all these tools demonstrated that there is more than one way to grab my slice of financial independence.

Nothing is set in stone. Over time, I began to realize that these tools were meant as guidelines. What works for one person may not be the same for another. There is no one rule that will give a magic number because your life is ever-changing and with each year a new piece of information comes to light.

EXERCISE: PREPARING THE "PERFECT FOR YOU" FI PIE

How do you want to build your income streams?

In Phase Zero, we talked about defining your *why*. Why do you want to be financially independent? Why start now? And we talked about setting some S.M.A.R.T. goals to get you started.

In Phase One, we talked about making the perfect FI Pie crust starting with four key ingredients: 1) calculating your net worth, 2) tracking your cash flow, 3) determining your credit score, and 4) cleaning up your credit history. With practice and time, work towards refining and evolving the crust to suit your FI Pie filling.

In this phase, the focus is on what you have within your control, namely, drawing on your own strengths and thinking outside the box to continually put yourself in a stronger position to reach financial independence. Daydream about all the different ways your FI Pie filling will be made, (i.e., all the different ways to earn passive income that you find interesting). Make a list. Then take some time to explore each one. Is it doable? Nothing is off the table. Right now, we are just exploring all the ways you could make your own FI Pie filling.

We all have different interests and tastes. What types of income streams will your FI Pie be made up of? Experiment and start building today.

PHASE **THREE**:
FI PIE FILLINGS

Be a first-rate version of yourself, instead of a
second-rate version of somebody else.

Judy Garland

As with many family recipes, there is a core list of ingredients and a set of directions. But to accommodate different tastes, there is usually a list of substitutions. This section is all about modifying the basic filling recipe to make your FI Pie recipe fit your lifestyle.

Up to this point I have talked about ways to spend less, invest more, pay off debt, and leverage the tools we have. With investing, I talked about never leaving money on the table by investing in the company 401(k), a Roth account, and a Health Savings Account. Most importantly, I talked about paying yourself first automatically and the power that comes with measuring cash flow against a home budget.

Understanding and mastering the basic recipe puts you well on your way to making the perfect FI Pie, but it's not enough. To be secure, you need to look beyond the basics and think about other ways to earn passive income, because life is uncertain. Markets crash and recover. Jobs come and go. Houses increase and decrease in value. Divorces and marriages happen. Babies are born. You get the picture.

Up to this point, my FI Pie filling was made up of cash investments, as in a rainy-day account, retirement accounts, and index type funds. In this phase, it's all about diversification. For me, that meant expanding investments into real estate as a new passive income stream and new FI Pie filling.

Income Streams: Passive and Active

What is an income stream? It is any revenue that comes into your life. This can be passive or active. Passive income is income that comes without actively working for it. For example, cash investments, dividend payouts, and rental incomes are common forms of passive income. Active income is what we actively work for. For example, a paycheck, side gig, and small business are common forms of active income.

At this point, I was disciplined in paying myself first with each paycheck, investing a percentage to my 401(k) and rainy-day fund before paying my monthly bills. But I knew I needed to diversify to mitigate risk. If the stock market dropped, what other income streams did I have to fall back on? To feel comfortable, I set a goal to have at least three income streams before quitting my day job. Since I was shooting for early retirement, I knew my retirement income streams from social security, 401(k), and IRA, would not be available for a while.

During this phase, I continued to consistently invest in my 401(k) while looking to start investing in rental properties. If there was a downturn in the markets, I would have rental income to fall back on whether markets were going up or down. Ultimately, after all my research, this was where my comfort landed.

My FI Pie filling would be broken up into three buckets, 1) retirement cash investments such as 401(k), IRA, and ROTH, 2) traditional cash investments such as index type funds, and my rainy-day account, and 3) rental properties.

What will your FI Pie filling look like?

YEAR FIVE: MY FIRST TIME

This year felt different, like Nina Simone's Feeling Good kind of different.

Yes, I started the year on unemployment, again. And yes, I had been recently diagnosed with Hashimoto's. In the process, I racked up about $10,000 in medical expenses. But I was standing on solid ground having done my research on real estate. I felt confident because I knew I did everything I could think of to start this new venture. That was empowering. I was feeling good because I had a plan.

My first order of business was to meet with the lawyer my tax accountant recommended. Together, we created my very first LLC for my rental property venture. It cost $650 to process the paperwork. Yes, I could have created the LLC myself, but decided to go with a lawyer for peace of mind in knowing that it was set up correctly. It was worth every red cent. (Check your state for the LLC filing fees. The prices can vary widely based on where you live.)

With the previous year's taxes in hand, I went back to the bank and met with the loan officer to get preapproval for two rental property purchases that year.

The loan officer had me fill out additional paperwork and put together a package to submit to the commercial loan office. Before I left his office, he told me to not get my hopes up. On paper, I was a single income earner with a temp job, a modest sum in investments, and half my home paid off. The bank was conservative in its lending practices. Even with excellent credit, my finances didn't look all that impressive. But I didn't care. As I walked out of the branch, I could hear Nina singing in my head, and I sang along with her.

I was on fire and believed nothing could stop me. I took every precaution, mitigated every known risk, and even talked to every person on my team one more time, going through all the questions and answers to stress test my plan. I was ready to begin this journey of building my very own rental property portfolio.

I waited on pins and needles to hear back from my loan officer. The weeks felt like months. Finally, it happened. I got the call from the loan officer to come in, my paperwork came back.

I walked into his office, sat down, and he got right to the point. My loan request for preapproval was rejected. I was crushed, he was not surprised. Without that preapproval letter there was no way I could put my plan into action. In complete and utter disbelief, I decided to do the only thing I could do: make my case.

I reiterated that I was a good risk for the bank, even though on paper it did not look like it. He pointed out the lack of monthly income and reminded me that a temp job did not count as income since it was unstable. They did, however, include child support as income. I explained that made no sense as child support would only be paid so long as my children's father had a job and, by definition, that was also "unstable". Even though the loan officer agreed, he reiterated that these were the parameters we had to work with. On paper, the only "income" I had was child support.

I reminded him of my years as a bank customer without even so much as one overdraft or bounced check. I also cited my excellent credit, paying all my bills on time and in full, showing my credit history report. I reminded him of my solid reputation for follow through and that I would not "make him look bad" if he would go to bat for me and resubmit my paperwork. Lastly, I told him if he did not feel comfortable to resubmit based on my say so, to discuss the matter with the branch manager, whom I had built a solid working relationship with over the years.

We went back and forth for a while. He sat there and politely listened to everything I had to say. In the end, he agreed to discuss the matter with the branch manager and would call me later.

The next day, the loan officer called to let me know he talked to the branch manager and decided he would resubmit my paperwork to the commercial loan department. Only this time he would hand the paperwork over to the commercial loan manager directly and make the pitch that I was a "good risk".

This process took a few weeks, mainly because the commercial loan manager was so busy it was difficult to get any of her time. Every few days, I would call to check in and reminded him (in the most professional way) that the decision was extremely important before I could move forward, and I would not let it go.

While waiting, I continued to do my research on available rental properties in different neighborhoods. The neighborhoods I decided to target were ten minutes outside of the downtown area and bus friendly. These neighborhoods were labeled up and coming, which is code for cheap houses in disarray and currently in not-so-great areas.

My Realtor set up a search agent that emailed me a daily list of what was available in these targeted areas. She knew the neighborhoods well, from building her family's own real estate passive income stream.

My loan officer finally called me back and asked me to come in. As I sat in his office, he started by saying he had good news and not so good news. First the good news, I was preapproved to purchase my first rental property. The not-so good news? The loan would only be enough to buy one rental property that year.

I wanted to know why I couldn't buy the first rental property with cash from the HELOC? Then I could turn around and use the preapproved loan for 80% and pay off the remaining 20% balance and do it all over again? That would demonstrate to the bank how responsible I am, right?

"It doesn't work that way," he replied. He explained that I was approved for only one rental property purchase because, according to my tax returns, I didn't have enough equity to purchase more. He advised me to come back the following year and resubmit my paperwork, with my new tax returns demonstrating newly minted rental income. If I could do this, it would support my case of purchasing another rental next year. Maybe even two.

I was disappointed and reminded him of my goal of purchasing two rental properties per year, starting that year. All he did was shrug and say, "there is always next year."

I had all this momentum that suddenly felt like it came to a crawl. I went home and sulked for a little while. I eventually regrouped and got over myself. I thought about all the things I had accomplished in these few short years.

What I realized was, it wasn't the "only being able to buy one rental property" that I was upset over. I just felt so far behind in my journey to financial freedom having floundered for most of my life. Was I ever going to catch up? Was financial independence just a pipe dream?

With a list of potential properties in hand, I did several viewings, walking through them, and making a list of repairs and costs. The real estate adventure was finally beginning. With each property I kept two things in mind to help me determine if a property was worth making an offer.

The 1% Rule of Real Estate

To help manage the list of properties, I used the 1% Rule. I multiplied the purchase price by 1% to determine the minimum monthly rent. If there were repairs to be made, I needed to add that to the purchase price. If the property could be rented for more than 1% of the purchase price, I would add it to the list of properties to visit.

Price Per Square Foot

The price per square foot is calculated by dividing the purchase price of a home by the square footage. It's a great way to compare a property to the rest of the properties in the same neighborhood. As a rule of thumb, buying the house with the highest cost per square foot, leaves you with the least room to make improvements as the value of the home does not usually increase with the cost of making repairs or remodeling. For this reason, it's best to look at properties that are the least expensive or in the midrange of the neighborhood. This allows some flexibility to make repairs or do remodeling and still have time to make your money back.

I am sure you have heard the expression, "cash is king." ... or queen in this case. That couldn't be truer in real estate deals.

Property Number One: Cash Is Queen

By the spring, my Realtor's search turned up a 960 square foot single family home with three bedrooms and one bath just ten minutes outside of downtown and on the main bus line. The list price was $79,900. It was in good condition, move-in ready, and just needed a new roof and HVAC system within the next few years (which gave me time to save up). I'll admit, I was nervous when I put in my offer of $67,500 all cash, or roughly $70.31 per square foot.

It didn't take long for the sellers' Realtor to let us know that we were one of two offers, for the same amount. The only difference was mine was all cash which allowed me to close two weeks earlier than my competition.

This was exactly the kind of scenario that gave me a leg up over the other offer. I had cash in hand because of my HELOC, which allowed me to skip all the extra loan paperwork. Selling to me would be easy and quick. The seller did not need to worry about the loan falling through. The seller did not need to wait a month, or longer, to close the deal and get their money. Selling to someone with an all-cash offer was like money in the bank.

A couple more days passed, then I got the call that my offer was accepted. I purchased the property for cash with my HELOC.

As planned, the very next day, I went to my loan officer and used my preapproved loan to finance 80% of the purchase price, or $54,000. Even though I paid the money out of my HELOC, I preferred to have that rental home mortgaged so I could free up the cash in my HELOC again. That left a remaining balance of $13,500 on my HELOC. My next order of business was to pay off the HELOC balance as quickly as possible to 1) incur as little interest as possible (tax deductible), and 2) prepare to purchase more rental properties next year for cash.

I hired a property manager and paid him $80/month plus maintenance and repairs. The property was rented out a month later for $850/month. Both my Realtor and property manager discouraged me from paying $80/month to manage only one property. They felt it wasn't worth the expense and instead offered to teach me how to manage it myself. But I insisted and promised to add to the portfolio next year to make it worth the money spent.

I am good at a lot of things, but managing property is not my strong suit. I am too soft. Left on my own, I would fall for every sob story about why rent could not be paid that month. Besides, I was too busy with a day job, family, and searching for the next rental property.

In hindsight, I regret not taking my property manager up on his offer to teach me how to manage rental properties. Hands on learning would have been invaluable. If I could go back, I would have taken him up on his offer and managed at least the first one.

In the spring I started a new 18-month contract job. But if the past had taught me anything it was that unemployment was *always* just around the corner.

With the purchase of my first rental behind me and starting a new contract, I had the second half of the year to take a breather. Honestly, I had been going strong for so long I hadn't noticed how run down I was. This was the perfect time to slow down. While I settled down in a new temp job, I also took some time to regroup.

I took a step back and reevaluated my rental property portfolio plan now that I had actual experience. It was becoming clear that buying ten rentals in five years might be a bit more than I could take on. Not because I didn't have the drive, but because I was missing some critical things in my original number crunching. Things like:

1) Paying off the 20% HELOC balance took longer than I originally anticipated.
2) I didn't factor in repairs while buying more rentals. It is true that this first rental did not need much in the way of repairs, but soon it would need a new roof and HVAC, which I budgeted $10,000 for both. This money would take away from the down payment of future rental properties. My first mistake.

Tracking Cash Investments

I also fine-tuned my method of recording the cash investments, my first streams of passive income. Instead of updating the totals every so often, I added a section to my budget tab on Excel and listed all my cash accounts under three categories: retirement, nonretirement, and other (529's, rainy-day, checking, and savings). At the end of each month, I started to consistently record the balance for each of the accounts. This gave me a very good idea of how the investments were doing and if I needed to rebalance the accounts. Go to **GrabYourSlice. com** and signup to get a copy of the Cash Investments Tracker delivered to your mailbox.

Before the end of the year, I also managed to pay $10,000 in medical expenses (my health insurance was not the greatest), continued to pay myself first, take a family trip, occasionally went out to eat, and generally just enjoyed myself. I was content and didn't feel the need to shop for things like I once did.

Being content gave me peace and a sense of happiness and pride where instant gratification once lived. I was accomplishing things I never thought I could. I realized that with focus on and commitment to investing, I was closing the gap on becoming financially independent. My FI Pie filling was starting to take shape with my newest passive income stream.

> *"Nothing is Impossible. The word itself says—I'm Possible."*
> **Audrey Hepburn**

My Steps for Creating a Rental Property Foundation:

- ☐ Established LLC for rental property purchases.
- ☐ Verified the Home Equity Line of Credit (HELOC) and was ready to purchase rentals for cash.
- ☐ Filed taxes early to obtain bank loan preapproval for rental purchases.
- ☐ Reviewed daily listings of new available properties using the 1% rule. (The minimum monthly rent needed to break even is 1% of the purchase price and repairs.)
- ☐ Scheduled time to visit potential rental properties.
- ☐ Bid on selected property.
- ☐ Used the HELOC to purchase rental property for cash, ensuring quick closing.
- ☐ Set up a mortgage for 80% of the purchase price of the new property.
- ☐ Paid off HELOC balance that is the remaining 20% of the new property purchase price.
- ☐ Listed property for rent.
- ☐ Reviewed applications.
- ☐ Completed needed repairs before new renters moved in.

❏ Went back to daily review of new available properties for next property purchase.

Entrepreneurs should always aim to play the long game. Instant gratification cannot build a legacy.
Andrena Sawyer

Lessons Learned

- Don't get discouraged by setbacks. Instead, think of them as learning opportunities to grow and stretch.
- Achieving financial independence takes focus, strength, and perseverance. Play the long game.
- I can have everything I want, just not all at the same time. Sacrificing a little now is starting to show how it will pay off down the line.

Year End Summary

Everything I had read about and practiced during the first four years led me to this moment of opportunity. This was the first year I was starting to see the fruits of my labor. My net worth was finally starting to show signs of improvement with a 34% overall increase. This was in part due to the first rental property added to my FI Pie filling. But it was also because my retirement accounts, 401(k) and IRA, totaled over $100,000 for the first time. My home checking and rainy-day accounts took a small hit. And I was still able to stay on top of debt incurred due to medical bills and the 0% credit card I opened to get my new home in order. I learned a lot this year which put me in a stronger position for the next few years. To see details, go to **grabyourslice.com/year-five**.

YEAR SIX: BUILDING A RENTAL PROPERTY PORTFOLIO

The prior year was a slow start to my original plan of purchasing two rental properties per year, but a start, nonetheless. With some experience under my belt, the new year presented me with more opportunities as I continued to grow my net worth and moved closer to my definition of financial independence (i.e., having enough money to pay my bills and take a trip or two). The hunt was on to find my next two rental properties.

I also still had my temp job and by the spring, I updated my resume and began reestablishing my job search with recruiters I had worked with in the past. I wanted to give myself plenty of time to find my next gig, hopefully a permanent position.

In the meantime, I kept up with my real estate research which put me in a great position to purchase my next rental property. With my newly filed tax returns in hand, I went back to the bank for a new preapproval letter. This time I was approved to purchase two rental properties.

Using the 1% rule, I created a list of potential properties to tour and found the next two rentals before summer ended.

Property Number Two: The Fixer Upper

It was a 900 square foot three-bedroom, one bath single family home listed for $60,000. Just like my first rental property, this one needed a new roof and HVAC system, but it also needed a ton of work, inside and out. The kitchen and bathroom needed an update, paint inside and out, new appliances, refinish the hardwood floors, new carpet in the bedrooms, new water heater, and new windows. The upside was it already had a renter, paying $650/month, which gave me time to save up for the list of repairs to be completed once the current tenants moved out.

Based on market conditions and other home sales in the area, I made a cash offer of $52,000 ($53.94 per square foot) with a short close. It was accepted right away. Why would I buy a property that needed all that work? Here's why:

1) I bought a whole house for $52,000 with a mortgage payment of $505/month for 8.5 years, in an up-and-coming neighborhood. This location could be worth a lot more over time and I could eventually increase the rent based on demand.

2) Most repairs don't scare me, but I drew the line at foundational work which this house did not need.

3) The home already had renters, which meant no down time.

4) Even at $650/month in rent, it was profitable.

5) After applying the 1% rule ($650 / $52,000 = .0125 or 1.25%) I realized there was room to do the work and later raise the rent after completing all the upgrades.

Just like the first rental property, I went right back to the bank and took out a loan for 80% of the purchase price.

Property Number Three: Picking Up the Pace

As I searched for my next rental, there were more investors hunting for deals in the same neighborhoods. I had more competition that I didn't have to deal with in the previous year. Cash no longer gave me the advantage it did with the first two properties since other investors were coming in with cash offers as well. I knew I had to stay vigilant if I was going to find the next one.

After looking at several properties, I came across one listed for $65,900. A 980 square foot three-bed, one-bath single family home also ten minutes from downtown and on a bus route. I put in an offer for $64,500 or $65.42 per square foot, which was accepted.

This third property needed about $4,000 in repairs mostly in the kitchen and bathroom before I could rent it out. It also needed a new roof and HVAC in the not-too-distant future. My rental property manager got his team to work on the repairs while simultaneously listing it on the rental market.

In the real estate business, time is of the essence. Every month a property is not rented is a month of lost revenue and a month of expenses you need to cover out of pocket. Fortunately, there was a lot of interest in renting the home. Again, I got lucky, as new renters moved in for $850/month within a couple of months of purchasing the property. My 1% rule was exceeded as the monthly mortgage was $622 on an eight-year loan. At a minimum I only needed $685/month in rent ($64,500 + $4,000 = $68,500 x 1% = $685/month). The excess would allow me to save for the roof and HVAC and pay down the HELOC.

Property Number One: Unforeseen Expense

While I was busy purchasing properties two and three, I started having issues with my first property. By the beginning of the year, my renters were not paying rent. They eventually moved out, but not before causing $2,000 worth of water damage in the laundry room. The repairs were made, and the property rented out after a couple of months. Not only did I lose the $2,000 in repairs, but also two months of rent. It was a hard lesson to learn that not every renter will treat your property with respect.

This was the kind of stuff I didn't have in my planning and was getting a firsthand education. I won't say I went into purchasing rental properties without realizing this could happen, but I wasn't going to let possible problems discourage me from building a real estate portfolio either. It's almost impossible to plan for the unknown. This was another mistake.

To mitigate my risk exposure, I did my best to keep extra rainy-day funds available just like I had for my personal household. But as a single income household, I was limited in how much I could set aside each month. Sometimes required repairs were paid on credit to my property manager. I would work hard to pay him back as quickly as I could. This was a deal I worked out early on in this venture.

But even with this agreement in place, all repairs were my responsibility. If I lost my job or rental income, I needed to know that I would be able to pay for repairs as needed. While I did my best to save up cash, I also knew that, in a pinch, I could use the HELOC to pay for things. This might cause a delay in my plans of purchasing more rental properties, but it was a risk I was willing to take. The benefits were much too great not to move forward.

Reevaluating and Next Steps

It was mid-year; I took a step back and reassessed my stretch goal of ten rental properties in five years. I had the next six months to pay off the HELOC balance while continuing to make repairs. It was a lot to juggle. Was purchasing ten properties a wise choice?

I pulled out my *why* (to make a better life for me and my kids where I was not dependent on a paycheck) and my overarching goal (to reach financial independence where my monthly bills are paid, and I could take a vacation or two each year). I read them both a few times and reflected in between each time. Was I still moving toward making my FI Pie? Each time I went back and reviewed my goals and *why*, I came back with yes, I am still aligned.

At this point, the rental market landscape was changing. There were more investors coming into the same neighborhoods with cash offers. This drove up the price of houses, making it more difficult to get the properties I wanted.

Ten might not be the right number but three did not feel right either. After doing some number crunching and talking to my property manager and tax accountant, I decided that next year I would purchase two more rentals and make a final decision on whether to pursue more or stop there.

Then there was my health and the Hashimoto's. I am not going to lie, it was stressful working at my day job, while building a real estate portfolio, and raising my two kids. I was in my 40s and laser focused on making up for lost time. All that pressure took its toll and racked up another $10,000 in medical bills within the year.

The year was flying by, and my 18-month contract was coming to an end. Even though I was proactive and diligent in my job search, I had nothing lined up. Unemployment was becoming a real possibility. Truth be told, I was okay with that. Yes, I had expenses and all of that, but I had been down this road before and made it work. I was in a much stronger position.

My boss called me into his office and asked me to take a seat. "Here we go again," I thought, expecting him to explain that my position would no longer exist, and he would hire me if he could but with budget cuts, blah, blah, blah. I knew the speech by heart. But he didn't say any of that. Instead, he told me the company was offering me a full-time job with benefits.

I was super excited. A full-time job with benefits, as in *real* health insurance!!!! I was over the moon. It had been a long road.

Finally, a permanent job and I could stop spending time looking for employment. Now was the time to really make my health a priority. With the permanent job came the opportunity to sign up for the HSA, but I didn't sign up for another three years. I talked about the Health Savings Account at length in Phase Two under How to Collect Free Money, so you can take advantage sooner than I did, should you decide to do so.

By the end of the year, my primary doctor gave me a referral to start working with a naturopathic doctor (ND). A naturopathic doctor heals your body by determining the root cause of the illness, then uses herbs and other natural remedies to heal and bring your body back in balance. This is *not* a plug for naturopathic medicine, but I had exhausted most conventional options and I needed to try something different.

I was physically exhausted and taking medication alone wasn't cutting it. I knew I needed to do more. No more shortcuts, I thought. Naturopathic medicine is the long road to healing my body. Ironically, now that I had health insurance, I couldn't use it, as naturopathic medicine is not recognized by insurance companies as *real* medicine. Nonetheless, I decided this was an investment in my health and needed to start taking better care of myself. Afterall, without my health, what did I have?

After the initial consultation and blood work, The ND and I had our first meeting to lay out a plan and timeline. For the most part, I had a decent diet. Even with that, she asked me to make some big changes and started with recommending I cut out gluten and dairy.

After the initial surprise, I agreed. Then she recommended giving up coffee, chocolate, and nuts. While I reluctantly agreed to give up gluten and dairy, negotiations kicked in when she mentioned the rest. Honestly, I thought I was going to get vitamins and herbs to add to my diet and not this complete overhaul.

I gave up the nuts, most of the time. But seriously, there was nothing that would ever make me give up dark chocolate. That was a non-starter. Dark chocolate was (and still is) my happy place. I mean, milk chocolate is mostly sugar, and white chocolate, well, that's not even chocolate. I wasn't eating either of those types anyway, so I joked that I would give those up. But to never eat dark chocolate ever again? It wasn't going to happen.

As for coffee, I compromised and switched to decaf, no sugar, no milk or creamer—a sacrifice that was easier to make than I thought. My morning ritual needs some form of coffee. My day is just not the same without it.

Okay, yes, part of me is being a little silly on some of this stuff. On the other hand, I was giving up bread, pasta, dairy (think ice cream people!), and caffeinated coffee for Pete's sake. The madness needed to stop somewhere. I drew the line at dark chocolate and black decaf coffee. That was a fair compromise and great starting point.

In all seriousness, we also agreed that I needed to bring down my stress level or the rest of these changes wouldn't amount to much.

Why am I sharing all this? True, it has nothing to do with real estate or financial independence. But it's important to understand that there is such a thing as *balance*. Too much of anything can be detrimental to one's health. I was so focused on rebuilding my life, that I neglected my health. And while I am proud of all I have accomplished, there are certainly changes I would make if I could go back. I would add in yoga, breathing exercises, walks, enjoying the here and now, and generally not taking life so seriously.

After almost two years of working with the Naturopath, I was in a much better place, with significant improvements in all areas of focus and even reversed some of the thyroid damage, resulting in lower medication.

"You must do the things you think you cannot"
Eleanor Roosevelt

Lessons Learned

- Perseverance and hard work pay off. Just remember to take care of your health. After all, without it what do you really have?
- Being a solopreneur requires a bit more checks and balances on the finances. Make sure to have rainy-day money and a back-up plan, like leveraging a HELOC.

Year End Summary

What a crazy, jam-packed year! I was able to purchase two more rental properties and grow my net worth by 31% overall. Most of the increase was in large part due to the property values, but my cash accounts did see an increase as well. Securing a permanent job made things easier to plan for ongoing property repairs as well as purchasing more units. With the job came 401(k) benefits that I maxed out to what the law allowed. But I did not take advantage of opening a Health Savings Account, a regret I have to this day. My rental property loans totaled to about $135,700, which is very respectable for three rental properties. Things were starting to come together. My FI Pie filling was growing and because I took the time to make a solid FI Pie crust, I could continue to increase my filling. To see details, go to **grabyourslice.com/year-six.**

YEAR SEVEN: RE-EVALUATING THE RENTAL PROPERTY GOALS

In Year Seven, the real estate market for single family home rental properties continued to tighten up. More buyers than ever before were joining the hunt and willing to pay cash. I needed to step up my game if I was going to lay claim on my next two rental properties.

Things were looking up. First, the year started with a permanent job (first permanent job in ten years), with benefits like health insurance and 401(k) with matching on the first 6%. I immediately took advantage of this (don't leave free money on the table) and I contributed the maximum the law allowed. Second, my health was in much better shape. Third, I owned three rental properties.

If I had to pick a theme song for Year Seven it would be Leslie Gore's, You Don't Own Me. It's such an empowering song! When I think back on that first conversation with the bank loan officer and how he thought my plan was nuts, well, I think it's safe to say, he was wrong.

Now armed with experience and actual numbers, plus the changing landscape of the housing market, it was time to set my goal for the year. Just like the last two years, I went back to the bank and got my preapproval letter to purchase two more rental properties.

All three rental properties needed work. At a minimum I needed a new HVAC and new roof for each. I leveraged the rent collected to start repairs. The first year owning rental properties, I broke even. The second year, I was in a small deficit. This was not the real estate empire I had heard so much about. When would I start *earning money on these properties*, I wondered? This was another lesson.

---

*Real estate is played for the long game
and not for instant passive income.*

The housing market continued to evolve with more investors and more competition resulting in fewer opportunities. I was committed to my plan of two more properties and in the up-and-coming neighborhoods originally identified. Owning five rental properties would justify all the work I put in.

Even with cash in hand and offering a short close, I was out bid on my next three offers and started to lose hope on finding my next investment. Two new properties were looking less and less likely this year. I dug deep and became even more determined to make my goal of at least five properties.

Property Numbers Four and Five: Section 8 and Doubling Down

Then in the spring, two properties came on the market that were perfect for me. Both had three bedrooms and one bath, about 1,000 sq feet, and both were about a ten-minute bus ride to downtown. I put a bid on both within a couple of weeks of each other. A gutsy move, even for me.

Rental number four came with renters and was labeled as Section 8 housing. (Section 8 is a federal program funded by HUD to make housing more affordable for low-income families, elderly, and the disabled). I purchased it for $60,100 ($51.06/square foot).

I quickly paid off 80% of the HELOC balance with a 15-year fixed loan at about $396 per month and chipped away at the remaining 20% balance making enough room to purchase rental number five for $60,000 ($59.39/ square foot) with the HELOC.

I lovingly call rental number five Doubling Down because I bought it two weeks after I bought the Section 8 property. It was bank owned and needed a fair amount of work before we could rent it out. None of the work was structural, so I was all in. My bid was accepted, and I quickly found out that the fair amount of work was going to cost about $20,000 to be move-in ready.

Now I had four separate rental property mortgages to pay, as the last rental, Doubling Down, was still on my HELOC and about $20,000 in repairs looming. Clearly, this was going to be another opportunity to grow and stretch.

Shortly thereafter, my property manager introduced me to a banker at a small local bank, who was willing to work with me on a consolidated loan for all five of my properties. He offered a 15/7 term fixed loan at 4.0% (A 15/7 means the monthly payment would be calculated for a 15-year loan but a balloon payment would be due on year seven).

If I went this route, I would end up saving on mortgage payments and could pay off the HELOC, which opened it up to pay for ongoing property repairs. The total loan would be for about $248,000. The only thing was, I would have a balloon payment after seven years of about $153,000.

In the end, after weighing the pros and cons, I decided to move forward with the consolidated loan. The savings each month was too good to pass up and my HELOC would be paid in full. I could fund the repairs easily. Besides, I could always refinance the consolidated loan down the road, which I eventually did.

With the decision made to move forward, I contacted the bank manager and asked to get started on the paperwork. It took a little over a month to complete all the rental property assessments and to get all the documentation together, but once I was approved and the consolidated loan was in place, I wasted no time getting to work on making more repairs.

I went from paying almost $2,500/month in mortgage loans to about $1,840/month with the 15/7 fixed consolidated loan at 4% interest. A savings of about $660/month or about $7,920 a year. Not bad at all. All five rental properties were rented out, bringing in an average monthly income of about $4,000 after I paid my property manager his fee of $400. To see a summary snapshot of the five rental properties, go to **grabyourslice.com/real-estate-calculations-sample-chart.**

Since interest rates were low, I also explored refinancing my primary home from the 30-year fixed at 3.75% to a 15-year fixed at 2.875%. Bringing my mortgage payment to $802/month from $788/month plus insurance and taxes. It was only a few dollars of savings per month, but I was shaving about 13 years off the life of the loan and saving thousands in interest.

It was a whirlwind year to say the least. A lot of big moves were made. But I felt good about all my decisions and my FI Pie was continuing to come together.

At the end of each year, I looked back to reflect on accomplishments but also identify what I could do better moving forward. As the year came to an end, I sat back and looked at my net worth, I couldn't believe the growth. For the past three years, I had been so busy building my portfolio, I hadn't really taken the time to fully comprehend or appreciate what I had accomplished.

For the first time in many years, I cried tears of joy. I was overwhelmed with a sense of pride, triumph, and, well, surprise. If anyone had told me seven years earlier that I would be the owner of five rental properties—and raising two kids all while on unemployment three times for a total of 22 months—I would have said they were crazy.

But here I was, feeling invincible, nobody owned me, and I had gained confidence that I could do anything I put my mind to. It felt amazing.

> *"Being defeated is often temporary,*
> *giving up makes it permanent."*
> **Marilyn von Savant.**

Lessons Learned

- Always make the effort to ask for something. The worst-case scenario is they say no and there is no change in your circumstances, but if they say yes, then all things become possible.
- Exercise your right to push your own limits. Not doing so robs you of the chance to know what you are truly capable of.

Year End Summary

It was another record-breaking year with not only my overall net worth reaching over $493,000, a jump of almost $97,000 from the year before, but my total assets reached an incredible $853,000. This was also a year of more firsts. It was the first time I had any experience with Section 8 housing. The first time I purchased a property that was bank owned. The first time I used a consolidated loan to pay off the four individual rental property loans plus the HELOC balance to make one affordable payment. This was also the first time I refinanced my primary home for a 15-year mortgage.

The credit card I opened back in Year Four was very close to being paid off and without incurring late fees or interest. This allowed me to leverage money towards building my rental property portfolio. On a smaller note, I bought a couple of individual stocks just to try my hand at it. More on individual stocks in Year Eight. To see details, go to **grabyourslice.com/year-seven**.

WHEN IS IT ENOUGH?

I stopped at five rental properties because each one I bought, while a solid purchase, needed repairs of one kind or another. Some needed additional repairs that I knew of, not to mention paying for things that I didn't know of and potential bad renters.

I knew for the next few years, all the rent collected would go to repairs and some of my paycheck would too. It took another three years to complete all repairs, major and minor, known and unknown. Maybe someday I will write another book called, *Adventures in Rental Properties*. So many stories, some funny, some not so much, but all of them had lessons and each experience increased my confidence.

These three years were whirlwind, exciting, and exhilarating and, at times, stressful but at the end of it all... very worth it.

Was it enough? I thought it was. After all, my goal was to generate enough income to pay my monthly bills and take a vacation or two. If it meant working part time to pick up some extra cash and health benefits, then I was good with that.

It was at this point that I realized my FI Pie filling was piled high and it was time to put my FI Pie in the oven. Just like in real baking, the pie goes in the oven with filling piled high but when it comes out, the fruit settles into a denser filling. Only time would tell if I was right. While it baked, I cleaned up my FI kitchen and thought about what was in my next chapter. Would my FI Pie slice be big enough to cover my modest lifestyle?

Rental Property Summary

Once I automated investing in my 401(k), I turned my attention to rental properties. At first, I did a lot of reading. I talked to my tax accountant and countless others who could give me invaluable insight into real estate. I spent time driving around recommended neighborhoods. I refined my FI filling recipe by adding in a rental property passive income stream.

All this research, as well as understanding my risk tolerance, helped to determine if this was the right kind of investment for me and my life. I also spent time determining if I were to go this route, how many properties would I need to make it worth my time?

While doing the research, I worked to put myself in the position to take advantage of opportunity when it came by. I did this by leveraging all the steps above, paying myself first whenever possible, and always being true to my *why*.

When the opportunity came to buy my first rental property, I was ready financially and armed with knowledge, grit, drive, and commitment.

I've created a checklist below to help guide you in buying your first rental property. For a PDF version go to **GrabYourSlice.com** and sign up for this checklist and more freebies delivered right to your Inbox.

- ❐ Do your homework. Read real estate books. (See recommendations at the end.)
- ❐ If you are still interested in real estate as a form of passive income, then ask yourself the following questions. These will give you a starting point on which to build:
  - o Do you have cash on hand to invest? Do you have strong credit?

o   Do you have a preapproval letter from the bank?

o   Do you have a Realtor that specializes in rental properties? This is critical as a Realtor can tell you neighborhoods to target and what a potential property can rent for.

o   Are you handy? Will you be making repairs or hiring out?
If you're not familiar with identifying needed repairs,
make sure you have someone you trust walk through the
home with you prior to the purchase.

o   Are you going to hire a property manager or self-manage
the properties?

o   Do you have a good tax accountant that is familiar with
rental property tax breaks?

o   Do you have a good relationship with your banker?

o   Are you willing to take on a fixer upper? Are there any
repairs you won't take on? For example, if a property
required foundational work, it was a hard pass for me.

❏ Talk to several Realtors with experience in rental properties.

❏ Talk with several banks to get a preapproved commercial loan.

❏ Build a cash nest egg to cover down payments, repairs (there
is always some level of repairs), taxes, and insurance.

❏ Stress test your budget to take on additional monthly expenses
like a rental property mortgage.

❏ Explore options to leverage other assets. For example, open a
HELOC against your primary residence.

❏ If you don't feel comfortable managing your own properties,
hire a Property Manager. Interview different companies or,
better yet, get a referral.

❏ Build a team consisting of a:

o   real estate agent that specializes in rental properties

o   property manager

o   tax accountant

o   financial advisor

o insurance company to discuss rates and different coverage costs

o handyman, roofer, plumber, electrician if you decide to manage your own properties

❏ Make a plan A, B and C then stress test them. What if...

o You lose a tenant? Can you pay the monthly expenses while looking for a new one?

o You lose your day job? Can you pay your monthly expenses?

o The tenant damages the property. Do you have enough savings to repair while potentially losing rent?

❏ If purchasing three or more rental properties, consider limiting liability by:

o Purchasing umbrella insurance.

o Establishing an LLC.

This list is not exhaustive by any stretch but meant to give you a head start in things to consider and understanding the amount of effort it takes. Do your own homework. Talk to others who have rental properties. Knowledge is power.

Cheerleaders and Nay-Sayers

I spent the first few years as a real estate investor building my team. These are my cheerleaders, advisors, and friends. They are honest and straightforward with good and bad feedback. These are the people I would lean on and who encouraged me to keep moving forward when I started to doubt myself.

One thing I have not talked about are the nay-sayers in my life. We all have them. These are the people that poo-poo all ideas that buck the norm of working and collecting a paycheck. They tear your dreams apart by saying things like "that will never work," or "you don't have what it takes." To be blunt, stop sharing your dreams with these people. It's a waste of your time, and your time is precious.

What I learned is that people who don't support you, or worse, tear you down, are the same people who are afraid. They want you to keep doing the same as they do. Why? Because if you do better, they have no excuse and know they could also do better.

What they don't understand is that change is scary for everyone. It takes courage to step outside of your comfort zone and to dare to do and be a better person than you were yesterday. It's easy to blame external factors that we have no control over instead of looking within and focusing on what we do have control over.

The bottom line is, if you really want something, put your mind to it, make a plan, persevere, and it **will** come together. It just takes commitment, grit, and the courage to raise your standards to what you deserve.

Know that you will make mistakes. What separates those that do versus those that don't is how those mistakes are handled. Are you the type of person that is going to get back up and keep moving forward? Of course you are, or you wouldn't have gotten this far in my book. Be amazing! Be all you!

EXERCISE: MAKE YOUR FI PIE FILLING

Up until now, the focus has been on lining things up to put you in the best possible position so when opportunity comes along, you are ready to take advantage. That is what Phase Zero, defining your *why*; Phase One, building your crust and taking inventory; and Phase Two, leveraging the tools you already have, are all about. You may have even given some thought to different FI Pie fillings. What would work for you and even what would not.

In Phase Three, the focus shifts to what makes up your favorite FI Pie filling. As I have mentioned throughout this book, what works for one person may not be the same for another.

My FI Pie filling was made up of retirement accounts, nonretirement accounts, a rainy-day fund, and now rental properties. That was what I felt comfortable with and I know the filling recipe well. Maybe your filling will look like mine, maybe not. There are lots of ways to generate passive income. With enough courage, grit, and perseverance, anything is possible.

By now, you should have a pretty good idea of what you like doing and what you don't. Maybe you have been spending some time experimenting in your FI kitchen with different types of fillings. Some filling recipes will be delicious, some may need a little tweaking before it's perfect, and some may be better left on the shelf. It reminds me of when my kids where little and I would occasionally slightly burn dinner. My son would say, "that's ok mommy, you made it with love."

That is how I want you to think about your FI Pie filling. Try your best. Experiment with different combinations. Sometimes it will be slightly burnt, but it will always be edible in terms of knowledge and experience and knowing what not to do next time.

If you haven't already tried a few FI Pie filling recipes, start now. Try different things and see what interests you the most. With each idea, and before committing money and time, start asking yourself:

1) What are my chances for success?
2) What can I proactively do I set myself up for success?
3) Do I need a team? If so, who would I need?
4) What are the risks?
5) How can I mitigate each risk?
6) What are the startup costs?
7) What are the annual costs?
8) How long will it take to implement?
9) How much could it generate conservatively?
10) How much could I lose if it doesn't work out?

Of course, this is not an exhaustive list of questions, but it should give you a good start in creating that FI Pie filling that is perfect for sustaining the lifestyle you want and deserve.

PHASE FOUR: IS THE SLICE BIG ENOUGH?

Somebody once said we never know what is enough
until we know what's more than enough.

Billie Holiday

The beginning of the year started much like the others. I reviewed last year's goals and mapped out new S.M.A.R.T. goals. There would be no purchasing of rental properties this year and no more additions to the FI Pie filling. My goals were primarily focused on rental property repairs and continuing the automated process of paying myself first in the form of cash investments. My FI Pie was in the oven. While it baked, those thoughts of doubt started to creep in. Did I forget an ingredient? Did I follow the directions and not miss a step?

About three jobs ago, I was in a breakfast club where we signed up to take turns bringing in Friday breakfast for the rest of the club. Not to brag, but I was one of the best in the rotation. Well, me and this other guy, who showed up with a full baked ham, but I digress. When it was my turn, I decided to pull out all the stops and made a sweet and savory spread that would win over the pickiest of eaters. One of the things I made was a breakfast cake. I got up early Friday morning to make it, and in my haste, threw the ingredients together, mixed it up, and quickly put it in the oven. As I was cleaning up the kitchen, I found three eggs on the counter and suddenly realized, my breakfast cake, now in the oven, had no eggs. There was nothing I could do except flip the oven light on and stare at the cake through the oven window, knowing full well I would not have it in my lineup. As I cleaned up my FI kitchen, I was similarly wondering whether I was going to find a missing ingredient, or two? Was my FI Pie going to be edible?

The imposter syndrome in me was strong. All I could do was stare at my FI Pie through the proverbial FI oven window. I reminded myself that my goal was to achieve financial independence and not retire completely. If I took on a part-time job, that would be fine. Or I could stay and work in my current job for a while longer. I realized that, for a change, time was on my side.

That was the beauty of making my own FI Pie filling, because it was a customized recipe, I knew that eventually it would be ready. Take for example, apple pie. It can be served cold or hot, with or without whipped cream or—my personal favorite—with vanilla ice cream. Keeping my options open helped to quell the feelings of doubt.

I was ready to take on new questions like:

- *When do I want to retire?*
- *What would that look like?*
- *How would I spend my time?*
- *Would I continue to work? If so, would I stay at this job or find something else to do?*
- *If I didn't work, how would I cover my expenses? And what would my withdrawal strategy be?*

For seven years of planning, perseverance, and grit, I had not given any of these questions a lot of thought. Now was the time to shift my attention. How long would my FI Pie stay in the oven? Achieving financial independence did not necessarily mean retirement from my job.

YEAR EIGHT: THE PIVOT YEAR

At the end of Year Seven my overall net worth was just shy of half a million dollars and total assets at just over $854,000. What I started to understand was having a net worth of a million dollars didn't really mean anything if I couldn't see how income would be generated. At this point, I wasn't clear how to make that jump.

Most of my net worth was tied up in the value of my home and rental properties. The other two buckets were retirement cash accounts that I consistently invested in but wouldn't be able to touch until retirement age. My nonretirement cash accounts, my rainy-day fund and an index fund, were fairly lackluster given my focus on rental property repairs.

With many repairs completed, some of the biggest ones were still ahead of me and I was still putting most if not all the rent back into the properties.

Mindset Shift

Besides not having the passive income to cover my personal monthly expenses, it turns out quitting a job with a steady paycheck would not be as easy as saying, "I quit". To make the move, I needed to change my thinking, from earning and investing to spending and managing assets. This was not as easy as I thought it would be, mainly because the way I have earned money for most of my life was through a paycheck. I knew this was going to be a big change.

In school, we are not taught to be free thinkers. Instead, our school system is set up to churn out more workers that depend on a paycheck and the benefits a job may give us. This was where my mind lived, and it would take some real effort on my part to undo that way of thinking and way of life. I started to realize that having the finances to quit was only half the equation.

I needed to evaluate what my future lifestyle would look like. What I realized was even if I had my streams of passive income lined up the way I needed it, it would take more than that to make me feel the euphoria of "I made it!". I completely missed the mark on what was next. What was I moving towards? I realized my goal needed to be more than an arbitrary net worth that I set years ago.

It boiled down to finding that balance between living a life worth reliving and making my investments last as long as possible.

Passive Income Streams

To help with changing my mindset on cash management, I needed to also do some basic math with the assets I did acquire.

Leveraging Rental Properties

My property manager and I continued to work together in prioritizing the final laundry list of known repairs still ahead. We guesstimated that all remaining major work could be done by the end of next year. In addition to that, I also controlled my expenses by lowering the mortgage and working with the insurance company to get the best deal. Lastly, something I neglected to add in my calculations was that rents would go up every year. A happy realization for sure. Finding the balance of expenses and rent would be a big factor in the passive income calculations.

Over the years, friends have asked why I use a property manager. At $80 per property per month, times five properties, times 12 months, this is a $4,800 per year expense. Aside from already admitting to being a softy and "too nice", there is a lot of paperwork to keep track of and I didn't want a call in the middle of the night for an emergency. All these things were not my strong suit. I knew if I took this over, it would be a costly mistake, much more than the $4,800 I spent per year. I knew my limitations, and with that, I made sure to add this expense in for future spending.

While my FI Pie was in the oven, I took a step back and made three new S.M.A.R.T. goals for the year. In this phase, it's not about adding to the filling but about making the slice that much more delicious. With that in mind, I came up with these three goals to achieve before I quit my day job, whenever that would be:

1) Have all known major and minor repairs completed and paid in full.
2) After all repairs completed, refinance the rental properties to lower the mortgage payments.
3) Have 50% of the rental income cover monthly expenses, in terms of mortgage, insurance, property taxes, maintenance, and property manager.

With these three new goals, and factoring in the annual rent increase, all gave me a very clear path to how I could improve my FI Pie slice once it came out of the oven.

Just like having a slice of pie for dessert, it's just better with a scoop of ice cream or caramel sauce or whipped cream or a combination of toppings. Sure, pie is great on its own, but better with a little extra.

Leveraging Rainy-Day Account

This was the year I had my first big emergency expense; the fixer upper property had a sewage backup from the main city line. It was early in the year, and we had snow on the ground. I put my tenants up at a hotel for a few days while the house was cleaned up. The front yard was dug up to replace the main pipe that connected to the city. It cost about $2,500.

We also had a big storm come through which caused damage to two gorgeous old trees in the backyard of the fifth property. I had no choice but to remove both trees for safety reasons. That cost about $2,900.

I also had one HVAC replacement, a repair of another HVAC, and various kitchen and bath repairs, costing about $5,300. All these repairs were on top of miscellaneous maintenance and upkeep costs.

Owning rental properties is work. Even with a property manager it can be expensive, especially buying fixer uppers.

To plan for a successful transition to financial independence and after all known repairs were addressed, how much should I keep in my rainy-day fund? This was not an easy question, but really, I felt comfortable with at least knowing that I have my HELOC to lean on, should that be necessary.

Leveraging Cash Investments

How would I know when I have enough cash in investments to reach financial independence? Even with the 4% Rule (the ability to withdraw 4% of total savings in the first year of retirement and adjusting for inflation every year after that), I still struggled to understand how that applied to me until I read Wes Moss's book, *You Can Retire Sooner Than You Think*. In it, he talks about his $1,000-bucks-a-month rule.

The $1,000-a-month rule states that for every $1,000 per month you want to have in income during retirement, you need to have at least $240,000 saved. Each year, you withdraw 5% of $240,000, which is $12,000. That gives you $1,000 per month for that year [for 20 years].
–thebalance.com

Wes' $1,000-bucks-a-month rule made things very clear. Not only could I clearly see how much could be generated each month, but how long it would last, based on when I started withdrawing income. From here I mapped out where income would be coming from, how much, and for how long.

This gave me a starting point of how my monthly expenses would be covered. As my FI Pie continued to bake, I became more and more confident that my slice would absolutely sustain my lifestyle.

My First Roth IRA

I talked about the Roth IRA and its many benefits in Phase Two under How to Pay Yourself First, but I did not take advantage of this tool until now. The first four years of this journey were all about learning the ropes of running my FI kitchen, building out my FI tools, and building out a strong FI Pie crust so when I made my filling, it would not fall apart. The next three years were a whirlwind with my primary focus on purchasing and repairing rental properties. It was easy to miss such an opportunity as a Roth IRA, since it felt like all my money was spoken for in some capacity. But it was a missed opportunity, nonetheless.

An Introduction to the FIRE Movement

This was the year I first learned about the Financial Independence/ Retire Early or FIRE Movement. It's not a new concept, but one that has made a resurgence. This new-to-me concept turned everything I was doing on its head. I didn't realize it, but all the work I had been doing to eliminate my debt and build my real estate and cash investment portfolio led me here.

A spark caught FIRE

Towards the end of the year, I came across a blog called DoughRoller. net, started by Rob Berger. If you are not familiar with the site, it's an excellent resource for those seeking better money management in all forms.

As I scrolled through his posts, I came across an interview with a blogger known as J. Money from BudgetsAreSexy.com. In the interview, J. Money talked about his own net worth and journey to financial independence. Curious by nature, I had to go over and check out the *sexy* side of budgets. Just like DoughRoller.net, BudgetsAreSexy.com is also an excellent source of information. More than that, J. Money made talking about money mainstream and comfortable. How does he do it? By being as authentic as anyone could possibly be.

Every month he dedicated one post to publishing his own net worth. Not only that but he listed his assets and liabilities, giving a play-by-play description of what changed that month and why, for better or worse. He does it all with ease and a wonderful sense of humor.

By the time I came across this site, he had already been doing this for a few years. It was all so fascinating, peeking into past months' posts. Being slightly competitive, I started to wonder how my own net worth measured up. These last eight years, I focused solely on paying off debt, collecting assets, and building my net worth. I thought retirement was something I would do in my 60's or 70's. It never occurred to me that retirement could occur much earlier.

Still, I was struggling with those bigger questions. *What does financial independence mean to me? How much do I really need my net worth to be to claim financial independence?* The more I learned the more my original goal of a million-dollar net worth became more and more vague.

The Basics of FIRE

FIRE or Financial Independence Retire Early, is a movement made up of people who front load their lives by making saving, investing, and building passive income a top priority starting at the beginning of their working career. When the passive income generated is enough to cover their monthly expenses, that's when financial independence is achieved and, as a result, early retirement becomes a reality. And when I say early, I mean retiring from corporate life in their 30s. They do this by using the 4% Rule as a guiding principle.

The question FIRE-minded people ask is: "Why work 40+ years then retire for 20 years when you can work for 10-20 years, and live life on your terms for 40+ years?"

Here's the thing, I started my financial journey in my early 40s. Clearly, I missed the "early" window. I just wanted to know with some semblance of confidence that at some point I could get to financial independence and retire. If I could fast track that goal, even better.

My parents lived by old money rules and always set aside a portion of their income every month and invested it, no matter what. They paid off their house and carried no debt. They lived below their means. Sounded like FIRE thinking to me. Oh, if I had only listened and learned from them early on, where would I be today?

After a little more research, I found a few FIRE books, one of them being *Your Money or Your Life* by Vicki Robin and Joe Dominguez. According to a *New York Times* article, Joe was able to live a frugal lifestyle by building a $100,000 nest egg and living on the interest of $6,000/year, allowing him to retire at the ripe age of 31 after years of working as a Wall Street stock analyst.

Like all strong movements, FIRE has evolved and over the years other flavors emerged, highlighting that there are different paths. There is no one-size-fits-all, even for retirement. For example, financial independence for a single person with no kids will look completely different from a married couple with two kids.

Then there is lifestyle to consider. Maybe the single person's idea of financial independence is taking a part time job and traveling versus the married couple that want to stop working and be home to raise their kids while still able to take family vacations.

Finally, it's important to look at how different locations will impact overall cost of living. In other words, financial independence in New York will be much more expensive than, say, Iowa.

Applying FIRE to My Life

What would my life look like without a day job and steady paycheck? That was the question I asked myself and thought about often. While the math part was clear, the psychological part of the equation was very real and very important to answer. I started with what I knew and came to several realizations.

1) I could, realistically, complete all the major rental property repairs within the next two, maybe three years.
2) Rental income would continue to increase.
3) Stock market always goes up over the long-term despite short-term ups and downs.
4) I needed to clarify how I would spend my time after my FI Pie was out of the oven.
5) I still wasn't 100% sure about the size of my FI Pie slice but I was always going to have that doubt, and just needed to take a leap.
6) I needed to know how I would cover health insurance.
7) I needed to know how I would replicate monthly income.
8) I needed to think about what had to be done before I quit my job. (To get this checklist and more freebies go to **GrabYourSlice.com** and sign up to have them delivered right to your Inbox.)
9) When I quit my job, I might lose much of my social network as many of my friends would still be working.

The expert in anything was once a beginner.
Anonymous

Lessons Learned

- Learning is life-long.
- To grow and stretch into the next chapter requires leaving the comfort zone.
- There is no amount of planning that will ever give a 100% confidence.
- Life is not lived in a straight line. That is why evaluating, and reevaluating life goals and lifestyle must happen often.

Year End Summary

In Year Eight, things started to slow down. No more adding to my FI Pie filling. I was done tweaking my personal recipe. My FI Pie was good enough to go into the oven. While I waited, I spent time focusing on what kind of toppings I wanted and what my next chapter would look like. How quickly could I claim financial independence? Shockingly, my total assets finished the year just shy of $1,000,000, which put my net worth at around $650,000. The credit card I opened four years ago to get my new home settled was paid in full and with no penalties or interest paid. My health was in good shape. My investments had good growth and things were moving along. It was a slower year, but one where I could see things differently and learned to change my trajectory. To see details, go to **grabyourslice. com/year-eight**.

YEAR NINE: THE ROAD TO FINANCIAL INDEPENDENCE

As in the previous year, my focus this year was to continue to repair, save, and invest. I continued to automatically contribute to my 401(k) up to the maximum and continued to tackle the list of repairs to the rental properties. I also learned more about the FIRE movement and how to apply it in my own life. Afterall, my FI Pie was in the oven. At this point, I just had to wait while my investments grew.

Looking back to the beginning of my journey, if someone had told me I would own five rental properties within three years, I would have thought they were crazy. Starting out, I was in six-figure debt, with a house and mortgage. I couldn't even secure a permanent job. But with courage, focus, and persistence, I accomplished more in the last nine years than I had in my first twenty years of adult life.

Adding FIRE to the equation only made it a game, to see how quickly I could achieve financial independence. I asked myself what else could I do to help with this overarching goal?

You remember that Health Savings Account (HSA) I talked about in Phase Two? I called it the triple tax threat. Well, this is the year I finally got around to opening one. And just like the Roth IRA, I regret not doing it sooner. I made a commitment that I would invest in the HSA and not spend any of it. My plan for this account was to bank it and let it grow until I am older, and my health requires a little more attention. This HSA would help offset the costs, in old age, or pay them off entirely.

Exploring New Hobbies

Over the years, I have had friends come to me for financial advice. They would ask me things like, how much do I need in my emergency fund? Or, what is the difference between the Roth IRA and an IRA? I found that I enjoyed teaching very much and started looking into other ways to teach financial independence. I had toyed with the idea of starting a blog for a few years, but the timing was never right.

I spent some time looking into the mechanics of what it took to start and maintain a blog.

Then I did something I normally would never do. I went to BudgetsAreSexy.com and emailed J. Money directly. I could count on one hand the number of times I have done something like that. But here I was, typing up an email to *THE* J. Money. In my email, I explained the divorce and the $255,000 debt, the downsizing, and rental properties. I told him I was thinking about starting a blog and asked if he had any advice.

For the record, I NEVER thought he would reply.

To my surprise he did reply, and quickly.

He was so encouraging and gracious. "Absolutely, yes, start the blog," he said. "You will meet so many wonderful people." He closed by congratulating me on my journey so far and sent me a link to a list of bloggers who were offering to mentor newbies like me.

After much deliberation, I decided to give it a try and came up with ThePieceOfthePie.com with tagline: Grab Your Slice (of financial independence). I bought the URL and started learning the ropes of blogging on WordPress.

I quickly realized I was in over my head and emailed three of the mentors J. Money sent me. Honestly, I wasn't sure what to expect. This was uncharted territory. Was anyone going to reply?

Sure enough, I got a response. That is how I met Doug Nordman aka Nords.

As of this writing, Doug was running the blog, the-military-guide.com and is the author of not one but two books, *The Military Guide to Financial Independence and Retirement* and more recently, *Raising Your Money-Savvy Family For Next Generation Financial Independence*. If you are active duty or retired military, his blog and books are for you. To all you military folks out there, I thank you for your service!!

Doug and I exchanged a few emails back and forth, and after an hour-long phone conversation he agreed to mentor me on this journey. I was over the moon excited about this new adventure and a little scared.

What I quickly learned was that starting and maintaining a blog really puts you out there. It's like that nightmare where you are on stage about to perform, you look down and -oops- you're naked. It took a lot of time to get used to it. Not to mention all the mechanics of blogging, which tools to use, and how to use them. Let's not even get into how long it takes to write a post. And then there were all the questions to figure out like, who is my audience, what voice would I use to be as authentic as possible, and a host of other questions I wrestled with. Doug was incredibly helpful with all these questions. We would brainstorm ideas on how to lay out each idea in a post.

I learned a great deal, no question. But I grossly underestimated how long getting a blog up and running would take. To really make a successful and profitable blog would take years and would be very time consuming. Nonetheless, I continued to play with my site and learned a lot about the mechanics of blogging, and that alone was satisfying.

Investment Club

I joined an investment club to learn the finer points of individual stock investing. I did buy a nominal number of shares in a handful of household-name stocks but picked them just to understand the mechanics and not because I had first-hand knowledge of the company's bottom line or growth plans. Most of my focus was investing in mutual funds. This, I decided, would be a great time to expand my knowledge of investing and really get into the guts of a company, understand investing terms, and how it all ties together.

I attended meetings for one year and found that I was no closer to understanding anything about a company's balance sheet. I also realized that while I love the planning for financial independence, that was vastly different from learning balance sheets and investing in individual stocks. I eventually sold any shares I purchased and put it all back into my mutual funds. No regrets though, this was a great learning opportunity and a stretch activity to get me out of my comfort zone.

Life Comes Knocking

One afternoon, mom called. She had just come back from the doctor and got the news that she had liver cancer, stage IV. The good news, it had not spread. They scheduled her for surgery, and I bought a ticket to go home for two weeks to help prep and stay that first week after the surgery.

The rest of that year, I flew back home as often as I could. I was falling behind at work and home. Balancing work and family in one state with my mom in a different state was stressful. After a long recovery, her margins were clear, and she was cancer free. From that point on she scheduled to see her surgeon every quarter. Each quarter she passed with flying colors. She talked about going back home to see her sister and the rest of the family for a couple of months as soon as she was back to her old self. It sounded like a great way to celebrate and was long overdue.

With mom on the mend, investments on autopilot, and property repairs mostly done, I had a feeling that the next year would be different. Watching my mom go through her health issues reminded me how short and precious life is. Maybe next year my FI Pie would come out of the oven.

By the end of the year, the blog was a just a skeleton. I was learning a lot and enjoying it. It turned out writing posts, editing, making them pretty, and emailing them out is very time consuming. It was not at all what I expected. But I enjoyed it even if only a handful of people were aware of its existence.

Running Retirement Scenarios

I didn't run retirement scenarios right away in my journey; maybe I should have. It could have been one more tool to leverage and keep me on track. On the other hand, I knew I was years away from being financially independent so why put energy into this tool? That was until I learned about the FIRE movement. Either way, it didn't really matter, the important thing was I was doing it now. If you haven't performed a Google search on Retirement Scenario Calculators, well, you are in for a shock. There are tons of them. Some are too simple, giving useless information. Others are too complex.

The best retirement tool to use is whatever-you-feel-comfortable-with and will use proactively.

Was my slice big enough to quit my job? My FI Pie was still in the oven, still baking. While I could smell the aroma that made my mouth water, the truth was I was not ready to take it out. There is a difference between moving away from something and moving towards something. I had time on my side to figure out what I was moving towards.

Food for Thought

By this time, I had built three income streams: cash investments, retirement investments, and real estate. I had a solid rainy-day fund and a newly added Health Savings Account. Because of my experiences, I am a believer in having three or more passive income streams. In other words, don't have all your eggs in one basket. This was my path to financial independence, what my FI Pie filling was made up of, but it doesn't have to be yours. My story is just one example. There is no one-size-fits-all.

I wanted to share my story because I wanted you to know that even with obstacles, setbacks, and challenges, financial independence is a reality for anyone with enough commitment, courage, and grit.

When I look back, what I know to be true is at the beginning of this journey, I did not know how to manage $10.00. How could I have possibly known how to manage $100 or $1,000? I started small, mastered that level, then moved to the next. That was part of the process of building a solid FI Crust and one that cannot be bypassed.

Remember to take time to celebrate the wins. Enjoy time with your family and friends. In the end it's not the stuff we have accumulated, but the memories we have made along the way that matter the most. Whatever your path to financial independence, have fun and treat yourself.

Life isn't about the destination but about the journey.

"Think like a queen. A queen is not afraid to fail.
Failure is just another steppingstone to greatness."
Oprah Winfrey

Lessons Learned

- Master the basics of making your FI Pie Crust. Having a solid crust will not only carry a lot of filling but it can carry many different types of filling.
- Hindsight is 20/20. In looking back on this journey, I could see that I had the right tools all along to build my perfect FI Pie recipe.

Year End Summary

In Year Nine, I played some major catch-up in a short period of time. It's amazing what can be accomplished with the right motivation. By the end of this year my total assets crossed the $1,000,000 mark and my outstanding home and rental property mortgages were steadily dropping. My cash investments continued to grow, and I finally added a Health Savings Account to my list of assets. I also learned that I don't like reading company financial sheets.

Was my slice of FI Pie big enough? Maybe, but it didn't matter because at the end of the day I was not ready to move to my next chapter. I was still getting my head around what I wanted to do next and what it meant to me to be financially independent. Because of this, I decided to leave my FI Pie in the oven for a little while longer. To see details, go to **grabyourslice.com/year-nine.**

While all these things were great, the most important thing this year had nothing to do with money or security. The most important thing was that my mom survived liver cancer and that was incredible.

EXERCISE: IS YOUR FI SLICE BIG ENOUGH?

To determine if your FI Pie slice is big enough to support your appetite requires a two-step exercise. Step one is to determine what your expenses will be now, and in the future. Step two is to analyze the various income streams and determine if it is enough to live on.

For this exercise, you'll need the following pieces of information:

☐ Your average monthly household expenses.
☐ List any upcoming big expenses within the next five years and total that up to put that amount in your rainy-day fund, plus a little extra.
☐ Your FI target age, or when your FI Pie will come out of the oven. If not sure, be conservative and pick the age at which you would like to be financially independent.
☐ List all income streams and average monthly amounts. For cash investments, use the $1,000-bucks-a-month rule.

Step One: How Big is Your Appetite?

Remember my goal was to have enough to pay the monthly bills and take a vacation or two. That was the size of my appetite. So, my FI Pie slice had to be big enough to cover that.

Now that you have been tracking your spending for a few years, you know exactly what your expenses are. Question is, what changes would there be in the future? As best you can, try to guesstimate what your expenses would be.

Some things to think about are:

- ❏ Would your mortgage be paid off?
- ❏ Would you quit your job? If so, there would not be a need for business clothes.
- ❏ Would you travel more?
- ❏ Would you drive less?
- ❏ If you have kids, would you pay for their college? Would they be living at home?

And so on and so forth. Just like thinking about what your life would look like to bring you joy, knowing how your life would change and how those changes would affect your bottom line are important in planning the next steps.

Step Two: Analyze Your Income Streams

Once you have all the pieces of information, total your income streams using the average monthly income you have coming in today. Is that enough to cover your monthly expenses? If you do, congratulations! Feels good, doesn't it? If you don't, how will your income streams change in the future? Will they increase or decrease and when will those changes happen?

I did this exercise many times before I was finally comfortable with the numbers. What is important now is that you are paying attention to your future life and can see clearly where you need to invest more time to get the budget just right to support your lifestyle.

If quitting your job is part of the plan, make sure to save up for all known big expenses coming in the next five years and add to your rainy-day fund. Does your rainy-day fund have enough to cover them all plus a little extra? If so, double congratulations! You are ready to move onto Phase Five.

Carefully take your FI Pie out of the oven, let it cool, then serve yourself a big fat slice.

PHASE **FIVE**:
SERVE AND ENJOY!

There is no greater gift you can give or receive than
to honor your calling. It's why you were born.

Oprah Winfrey

YEAR TEN: A BEAUTIFUL DAY

The year started off great! My mom was cancer free and feeling good. My total assets had just crossed the one-million-dollar mark. The real estate market was hot and property values were on the rise. My retirement investments also hit a milestone. My 401(k) crossed the $100,000 mark, in four years. This was due to multiple factors:

1) contributing the maximum
2) leveraging paying myself first consistently
3) investing in a stock-based fund
4) collecting the company match

I continued to automatically invest through paying myself first every month. Doing that paid off in spades not only in my retirement accounts but in my nonretirement accounts as well.

As for the rental properties, most of the major, known repairs were behind me. I could start to see a light at the end of the tunnel. But I still had the two biggest repairs ahead of me.

Property number four, the Section 8 property, needed to be converted to a regular rental and the dreaded property number two, the Fixer Upper, needed a new everything.

To get these two properties the needed repairs, the renters would need to move out. This was something I continued to drag my feet on (and that would cost me). I wasn't looking forward to ending the now month-to-month lease I had with both tenants. This was also why I would never make a good property manager.

The overall big picture of my finances looked great. I was a long way from my starting point, and it felt good.

Every year since I started on this journey, I had one focus, and one focus only: *To never depend on a paycheck.* My original goal was to generate enough passive income to pay my bills and take a trip or two. I realized that even though I was lightyears away from my starting point, I didn't feel any different. I couldn't say for certain that my slice was big enough because I still had not decided on what my next chapter would look like.

Besides, I still had two major rental property repairs I needed to complete. Having a paycheck would make those repairs easier. Sure, it wasn't the only way to handle the repairs, but it was the way I felt most comfortable handling them.

A Word About Debt and a Home Mortgage

*Every article I had ever read about retirement
included in the checklist that <u>all debt must be
paid in full</u>. Did that include my home mortgage?
Some say yes, others say no with an asterisk. The
mortgage was not a deciding factor in determining
retirement as long as enough passive income was
generated to cover the mortgage payments. Some
added in a rule of thumb that if the mortgage
loan was not paid in full at the time of retirement,
it should be paid off within the first five years of
retirement. This, I am guessing, is to make sure there
is income available in the golden years, should there
be unforeseen health issues or major expenses.*

> *So, a new question came up: Should I pay off*
> *my home mortgage before I quit? Am I adding*
> *new goals for the sake of avoiding leaving a*
> *safe paycheck? Was fear creeping back in?*

When thinking about my life's next chapter, I like the way author Dr. Ruth Westheimer put it in an interview when asked about retirement at 93 years young. She said, "I will never retire, I rewire." That resonated with me. Why sit still when there are things to be done? One thing was for certain, I didn't want a 9 to 5 desk job in my next chapter, but I still wanted to be working in some capacity. In my next chapter, I decided I would be working on passion projects that may even generate income.

Breaking Down Passive Income

Based on the first book I read about passive income, *You Can Retire Sooner Than You Think*, by Wes Moss, he had a $1,000-bucks-a-month rule for early retirement and a 5% rule for withdrawing funds. But the FIRE community had a 4% Rule.

Between Moss's rule and guessing that we were roughly spending about $3,500 a month at the time, I did some quick math. What I realized was if I had about $2,000 in rental property income, I could get away with $1,500 in income from non-retirement investments. This meant I needed a minimum of $480,000 in non-retirement investments plus extra cushion in my rainy-day fund.

Knowing when I could access different buckets, how much per month each would generate, and how long it would last, was starting to paint a picture.

Turning my attention back to the rental property passive income, I did some quick math to list all the known expenses such as mortgage, insurance, and property taxes as well as property management fees. If I had full occupancy and no major expenses, I could clear about $1,700 a month.

I knew that over the years the rent prices would go up as I continued to pay down the consolidated loan. Down the road, I could refinance it before the balloon payment came due and lower my overall monthly payment while extending the terms of the loan. I kept my options open and leveraged what made the most sense and at the right time.

Life Comes Knocking - Part II

Early in the year, my mom went to the doctor for her quarterly check. After getting her results, she called to tell me that the cancer had returned, and this time it was very aggressive. I couldn't believe it; I was in shock.

Since I had Power of Attorney, I called her surgeon myself and asked what going on. I thought maybe mom had misunderstood. But she hadn't and I found myself struggling to accept the difficult truth. His advice was to take her to visit her family as soon as possible, while she was still healthy enough to travel. The news hit us all hard. I couldn't understand how she could go from *on the mend* and *cancer free* to having the cancer come back so aggressively.

It was a hard conversation to have with my mom. We talked about that trip to visit the family. I told her we could go together, like we used to when I was a kid. It would be a family trip. But she had no interest in going anymore. She didn't want anyone to know. She insisted on staying in her home. No hospice. We did what we could to accommodate that request. Four short months later, she passed away.

It was hard to understand or believe she was gone. I would tell myself that at least she was not suffering anymore.

Looking back on this time, I learned that there is never enough time to spend with someone. All any of us can do is our very best. She passed away and I never did tell her how I had turned my life around, that she didn't need to worry about me and the kids because I had built a strong financial foundation that included security. All of it seemed so pointless.

Months had passed and I bought myself a ticket to attend a financial conference. It was recommended by both Doug and J. Money. After the loss of my mom, the conference was a welcomed distraction. I met like-minded people, made new friends, learned a lot, and started collecting ideas about how I wanted my next chapter to look. It was a whirlwind few days and a ton of fun.

After that conference, I was inspired to try my hand at blogging again. This time I started by emailing a larger pool of friends and asking if they would support me in this activity by allowing me to email them weekly posts. A handful of people replied, and it was enough to get me started in shoring up a weekly routine and process. (Many thanks to my friends and family for all your support in those early months. You know who you are!)

As for my own definition of financial independence, by the end of the year, it was very clear the numbers on paper were only part of the story. The bigger, more important piece was knowing that I am the person I want to be. That means I am the best mom I know how to be, I am a good person, and I have security that lets me sleep at night. I know I will work until I am physically unable to because, really, that is part of who I am. The only difference is now I work on projects that bring me happiness and contribute to society in a positive way. And I work when I want to.

None of us know how long we will be on this earth. Every day is a gift. Being on this journey has been a holistic one that was about more than money in the bank. That was the biggest lesson of all.

Your time is limited, so don't waste it living someone else's life. Don't be trapped by dogma—which is living with the results of other people's thinking.
Steve Jobs

Lessons Learned

- Don't focus so much on the goal that you forget the people you know and love around you.
- The time to move to your next chapter is when you are ready. The numbers are only representative of the FI Pie recipe. What you do when the pie comes out of the oven is up to you.

Year End Summary

Here I am, at the end of this ten-year journey. I did achieve my net worth goal. I was, by my own definition, financially independent and served myself a big fat slice of my FI Pie. I didn't quit my job right away for personal and professional reasons. For one thing, I had professional goals to achieve and projects to complete before I felt comfortable leaving. Before leaving a job, my goal was to leave it better than when I got there. It's about doing the right thing, even when no one knows. I knew. My mom once told me, in life there are no rules except one. You need to be able to look yourself in the eye and be happy with what you see.

Besides, I needed some time to just be. This journey was a whirlwind. There was no need to rush to my next chapter. What was important was respecting myself enough to not push. I needed some time to sort things out because, well, my life was not lived in a straight line.

EXERCISE: WHEN TO SERVE AND ENJOY?

By now you have a solid understanding of your finances. In this last phase, turn your attention to planning out the steps to move towards your next chapter. It's more important to clearly define what you are moving towards versus running from something. Running from something is a single act. But then what? Taking the time to define what your next chapter looks like will solidify happiness and joy in your life. Planning your next chapter will get you excited to move forward without fear.

Eventually, you will be ready to quit your job. Before sending in your letter of resignation, review the checklist below. Go to **GrabYourSlice.com** and sign up to get this and many other freebies delivered to your mailbox.

Things to Consider Before Planning Your Exit

- ☐ Write your ideal *next chapter* job description. Be clear in your mind what you are going for.
- ☐ If you like your company but are bored with the current role, then think about internal options. For example, consider moving to a new department or division, or move to a new role within the same team.

- [ ] If you like your job but want more autonomy or some other perk, then talk to your manager about some changes you would like to see.
- [ ] Above all, make sure to be honest about why you want to leave and exhaust all options before making any final decisions.

One to Two Years Out

- [ ] Talk to your family about quitting, what that means, and how it impacts them.
- [ ] Talk to your family about your plan.
- [ ] Build 12-months of reserves.
- [ ] Clean up:
    - o Email, including sent and draft folders.
    - o All electronic files.
    - o Internet browser history.
    - o Software that was only meant for you.
    - o Office desk and shred documents as appropriate.
    - o Document all your achievements.
    - o Review all benefits and compensation. Keep copies of your annual reviews and any legal documents signed.
    - o Take all free training and certifications offered.
    - o Begin to think of when your last day will be so that you can collect all free money.

One Year Out

- [ ] Pay off all debt. Save up for any future major expenses and a little extra.
- [ ] Complete all major house projects.
- [ ] Complete all major medical needs.
- [ ] Refinance mortgage if needed.
- [ ] Research independent medical insurance.

❏ Begin to build a budget for after employment.

❏ Talk to your financial advisor about your plan and ask what to expect in terms of passive income.

Six Months Out

❏ Increase all credit card limits.

❏ Schedule all medical appointments including dental and eye exams.

❏ Fill all prescriptions before last day.

❏ Make a list of all work projects, status, team members, and anything else to help with the transition of workload.

❏ Update your resume and LinkedIn Profile.

    o   Ask teammates for recommendations and write some recommendations.

❏ Refine your *after-employment* budget as you learn more.

❏ Draft your letter of resignation.

❏ Plan a vacation for the first one to two weeks of freedom.

One Month Out

❏ Set a meeting to talk to your manager about your last day then email your letter of resignation to your manager and copy the Human Resources representative.

❏ Work with your management to make a work transition plan.

❏ Meet with your successor and make things as easy as possible.

❏ Verify that unused vacation days will be paid out and when.

❏ Verify when medical benefits stop.

❏ Complete all medical appointments.

❏ Continue to refine your *after-employment* budget, making changes as you learn more.

❏ Have a follow up meeting with your Financial Advisor:

- o   Verify that your financials are in order and will support your new lifestyle.
- o   Determine when to rollover your 401(k) to an IRA.
- o   Determine when to move your Health Savings Account.

Two Weeks Out

- ❒   Notify your teammates. Be humble and say thank you.
- ❒   Make sure to turn in all company equipment and get documentation on what was turned in.

Of course, the other half of that equation is making the leap when you are ready. Truly, only you can answer that. It is not uncommon for people to have a perfect-for-them FI Pie slice sitting right in front of them and achieving all their financial objectives only to discover they are simply not emotionally or mentally ready to take that first bite. For some, it may take a year or three. In this phase, there is no formula to follow. Listen to your heart. Only you will know when the time is right. And when you are ready, everything else will be in place just as you planned it (sort of).

WHAT'S NEXT?

What I now know to be true is: It wasn't about the "net worth of a million dollars". This journey was never about the money. Money is nothing more than a tool to get to a better place. Eventually, I quit my job. I did it on my terms and when it felt right for me. It was sad to leave behind many friends but also excited to start my next chapter. That really is all it is, a new chapter. All my major rental repairs were completed. I eventually refinanced my consolidated loan and kept my HELOC for potential future repairs should that be necessary. At work, I did my best to leave my teams in the strongest position possible. Everything fell into place.

In this next chapter, I switched careers and became an author, blogger, and financial coach (not in that order). The kids are grown now and off on their own life adventures. I travel some when I want to and spend time with friends. I have enough passive income generated to pay my bills and take a trip or two. Most importantly, I am happy and content in my life. I don't know what my future holds, but one thing I know for certain: I am going to be okay, no matter what life throws at me.

A question for you my dear reader. You now know my story, or at least a peek into this ten-year period. This is where my story ends and where yours begins. If you were financially independent, what changes would you make in your life? What are you willing to do to grab your slice of financial independence?

LETTER TO MY YOUNGER SELF

Dear Younger Me,

You are going to have a great life! I know because I am future you. 😊

Okay. Now listen up! Your life will be like a great movie, filled with laughter and tears, triumphs and disappointments, anger and joy. It won't be perfect, but, like all great movies, it will be worth your time, leaving you wanting to watch it again.

There are just a few "housekeeping" items I would like to share up front to save you (us) some time and heartache. Hold these truths close.

1) *You'll make mistakes. Embrace them.*

   Make them quickly and learn from them. Those mistakes are proof you tried. Even Thomas Edison learned 10,000 ways to *not* make a light bulb. Perseverance is your friend. If you want something, go get it. The truth is we are all just making it up as we go along. Don't let anyone tell you differently.

2) *Believe in yourself. Know your worth.*

   Be your own biggest cheerleader. People will treat you no better than the way you treat yourself. Give respect and demand it in return.

3) *Forget the Joneses.*

   Live life on your own terms and not for the sake of others. It's a waste of time trying to impress people that don't know you or appreciate who you are.

4) *Invest in yourself.*

   Learning is a lifetime affair. Open your mind to new things. Learn to negotiate. Learn to manage your money. If you can't manage $1,000, you won't be ready to manage $1,000,000. Take the time to understand what you enjoy and steer in that direction. Take chances and never let fear be a reason to not do something.

5) *Live below your means.*
   Know what you value. Living isn't about accumulating things; it's about accumulating experiences and living in the little moments. Get creative and discipline yourself to live on a fraction of your paycheck and invest in a Roth, 401(k), HSA, Rainy-Day Fund, and Travel/Fun Fund. Knowledge without action means nothing.

And most importantly...

6) *Spend time with family and friends.*
   Surround yourself with people who love and appreciate you for who you are. Be all you. In the end, you'll regret the things you didn't do more than the things you did.

So, there you have it. Simple rules to live by. Go easy on yourself. You are going to be amazing! Have fun!

APPENDIX A: LIST OF FIRSTS

Year One

- Started making financial security a priority.
- Started recording all income and spending.
- Learned from others further along on this journey.
- Defined my starting point by pulling my credit score and credit history and calculating my net worth.

Year Two and Three

- Consolidated my home mortgage and Home Equity Line of Credit (HELOC) into one loan.
- Did a mid-year analysis of my spending.
- Flexed my financial magician skills.
- Purged the house (traded stuff for money).

Year Four

- Bought first home on my own (downsized).
- Sold first home on my own.

- Continued to refine my goal setting skills.
- Traded-in my car and bought a secondhand Honda without a loan.
- Planned to build first passive income in rental properties.

Year Five

- Established Limited Liability Corporation (LLC).
- Received bank pre-approval for rental #1.
- Purchased first rental property and hired Property Manager.

Year Six

- Purchased rental #2 with renters (most expensive to repair) and rental #3.
- First permanent job in nine years.
- First introduction to Health Savings Account and when I *should have* opened one.

Year Seven

- Purchased rental #4 (first Section 8)
- Purchased rental #5 (first bank owned purchase), two weeks after rental #4.
- Consolidated four rental property loans and the balance on the HELOC into one loan.
- Refinanced home loan to a 15-year loan.
- Purchased individual stocks.

Year Eight

- Introduction to FIRE and concept of early retirement.

Year Nine

- Opened first Health Savings Account (HSA).
- Joined first investment club.

Year Ten

- Attended first financial conference, FinCon.
- Launched first blog, ThePieceOfthePie.com.
- Net worth goal achieved.

APPENDIX B: GRAB YOUR SLICE OF FI PIE CHECKLIST

Phase Zero: Pie? What Pie? Eat Everything!

- ☐ Define your *why*. Why now? Read daily.
- ☐ Set annual S.M.A.R.T. goals. Review and update daily.
- ☐ Make a list of future goals to pull from as needed or at least annually.

Phase One: Inventory and Assembling the Perfect FI Pie Crust *

- ☐ Calculate net worth annually.
- ☐ Record cash flow daily.
- ☐ Pull credit score at least annually.
- ☐ Pull credit history annually.
- ☐ BONUS: Record cash investments monthly.

Refine your FI Pie Crust recipe often.

Phase Two: Tools and Directions

- ☐ Identify areas to stretch your money.

o   Create a budget that supports your lifestyle and priorities.

o   Review your spending against the budget.

o   Adjust the budget as you progress and as your life-style changes.

☐ Boost your net worth instantly. Go back two Phase Two under Directions.

☐ Pay off outstanding debt, if applicable.

☐ Research and collect all free money offered.

☐ Begin to use money and budgeting as tools to leverage.

☐ Practice paying yourself first. Leverage direct deposit and invest.

☐ Begin experimenting with making different FI Pie fillings.

☐ Refine your FI Pie crust based on your perfect filling recipe.

Phase Three: Assembling the Perfect FI Pie Fillings

☐ As needed, continue experimenting with making different FI Pie fillings.

☐ Determine what your FI Pie will be filled with.

☐ Assemble FI Pie crust.

☐ Assemble FI Pie filling.

☐ Pull the FI Pie together and put it in the oven.

Phase Four: Is the Slice Big Enough?

☐ Review and refine, as needed, the lifestyle you want.

☐ While your FI Pie is in the oven, determine your slice size.

o   Determine how much you need to live on monthly.

o   For each income stream, list monthly cash flow, when it starts and ends.

☐ If your total monthly income streams are greater than your monthly expenses, take your FI Pie out of the oven, let cool then slice.

☐ Determine how long you want to continue in your current job.

❏ Begin planning your next steps.

Phase Five: Serve and Enjoy!

❏ Define your next chapter.
❏ If you are quitting your job, see the Before You Quit Your Job Checklist.
❏ Enjoy your next chapter.

APPENDIX C: LIST OF FREE RESOURCES

The following free resources can be emailed to you upon request. Go to **GrabYourSlice.com** for details.

Core Worksheets:

- ☐ PT 1 – Cash Flow Tracker
- ☐ PT 2 – Cash Investment Tracker
- ☐ PT 3 – Net Worth Tracker

Supporting Worksheets:

- ☐ Goal Setting Template
- ☐ Rental Property Tracker
- ☐ Debt Payment Planner
- ☐ Raising Credit Score Basics Template

Checklists:

- ☐ Before Purchasing Rental Properties Checklist
- ☐ Before Quitting Your Job Checklist
- ☐ Grab Your Slice of FI Pie Checklist

BIBLIOGRAPHY

Pie? What Pie? Eat Everything!

Lake, Rebecca (2020). "How to Achieve Financial Independence." *Smart Asset*, 5 Oct. www.smartasset.com/financial-advisor/financial-independence

Haughey, Duncan (2014). "A Brief History of Smart Goals." *Project Smart*. www.projectsmart.co.uk/brief-history-of-smart-goals.php.

Statista Research Department (2021). "U.S.: Annual Unemployment RATE 1990-2018." *Statista*, 22 Jan. www.statista.com/statistics/193290/unemployment-rate-in-the-usa-since-1990/.

Take Inventory and the Perfect FI Crust

Wallet Hub (2021). "Credit Score Range." *Wallet Hub*. wallethub.com/credit-score-range/.

MyFICO (2021). "How Are Fico Scores Calculated?" *MyFICO*, 4 June. www.myfico.com/credit-education/whats-in-your-credit-score.

Annual Credit Report (2021). "Annual Credit Report Home Page." *Annual Credit Report.com*. www.annualcreditreport.com/index.action.

Merriam-Webster (2021). "Budget." www.merriam-webster.com/dictionary/budget.

Tools and Directions

Black, Michelle (2022). "What Is the Average Credit Card Interest Rate?" *Forbes*, 5 Apr. www.forbes.com/advisor/credit-cards/average-credit-card-interest-rate/#:~:text=The%20Federal%20Reserve%20keeps%20tabs,that%20assessed%20interest%20was%2016.45%25.

FI Pie Fillings

Nowacki, Lauren (2021). "Breaking Down the 1% Rule in Real Estate." *Rocket Mortgage*, 27 May. www.rocketmortgage.com/learn/1-rule-real-estate.

Is the Slice Big Enough?

Hayes, Adam (2021). "Dollar-Cost Averaging (DCA)." *Investopedia*, 13 Sept. www.investopedia.com/terms/d/dollarcostaveraging.asp.

Roth, J. D. (2020). "We Didn't Start the Fire: The True History of Financial Independence." *Get Rich Slowly*, 13 Dec. www.getrichslowly.org/history-of-financial-independence/.

Goldberg, Carey (1997). "Joe Dominguez, 58, Championed a Simple and Frugal Lifestyle." *The New York Times*, 27 Jan. www.nytimes.com/1997/01/27/us/joe-dominguez-58-championed-a-simple-and-frugal-life-style.html.

RESOURCES

Books On Real Estate

- *Tax-Free Wealth* by Tom Wheelwright
- *The ABCs of Real Estate Investing* by Ken McElroy
- *Real Estate Riches* by Dolf de Roos

Books On Financial Independence

- *Automatic Wealth* by Michael Masterson
- *How Much Money Do I Need to Retire?* by Todd Tresidder
- *The Millionaire Next Door* by Stanley Danko
- *The Power of Less* by Leo Babauta
- *Wealth Can't Wait* by David Osborn and Paul Morris
- *You Can Retire Sooner Than You Think* by Wes Moss
- *The Simple Path to Wealth* by J. L. Collins
- *The E-Myth Revisited* by Michael Gerber

Blogs on FIRE

- DoughRoller.net, Rob Berger
- BudgetsAreSexy.com, J. Money
- The-Military-Guide.com, Doug Nordman

Other Resources

- SideHustleNation.com, Nick Loper
- Investment Risk Tolerance Assessment, University of Missouri
- Real Estate How-to Books, John T. Reed
- Annual Credit Report, Resource to pull your credit report for free

THANK YOU

Thank you for taking the time to read Grab Your Slice of Financial Independence. I hope you enjoyed reading it as much as I enjoyed writing it. Please take a moment to leave a review so other readers can discover this book.

I also want to thank all the beta readers that gave me feedback and supported this project. Thanks to Doug, who continues to mentor me. Thanks to my editors, M.K. Williams, and Sara Bruya, who were amazing to work with, shared a lot of great advice and patience. Thanks to Ashley Morrison of Abundant Marketing for helping with the web design and setup. Thanks to Denise Thornton who did an amazing job with my headshots.

Thanks to my friends who continue to support me in this crazy idea of publishing a slice of my life's journey to inspire others. I couldn't have done it without all of you.

Special thanks to my kids for being my cheerleaders, my significant other and life partner for accepting me as is, my mom for teaching me her financial magician tricks, and my dad for his occasional #kickintheass.

To stay connected or get more inspirational content delivered to your mailbox, you can subscribe to my newsletters at **GrabYourSlice.com**.

To get your free Financial Independence worksheets and checklists, visit **GrabYourSlice.com**. Once you sign up, all the freebies listed in Appendix C will be emailed to your Inbox.

ABOUT THE AUTHOR

Monica has 10+ years of experience through her personal FIRE (Financial Independence Retire Early) journey. Her financial "couch potato" watershed moment was when she realized she had $257,000 of debt. Ten years later, she achieved financial "rock star" status, having obtained Financial Independence (FI).

Monica is a mother, daughter, sister, friend, significant other, and Financially Independent Retired, or FIReD. When she is not writing or teaching financial independence, she is spending time with her friends, family, and kids (while they still want her around). She is also a first-generation American Italian with dual citizenship for herself and her kids. Most of her adult life, she has had pets around, having adopted two rescue tabby cats and two rescue beagles. She loves meeting people and hearing their stories and believes we are more alike than different.

https://www.ThePieceOfthePie.com/
https://www.GrabYourSlice.com/

9 798986 345512